THE RED BAG

CONNECTING THE JOURNEY OF HEALING THROUGH LIFE, DEATH & BEYOND

ALSO BY PAIGE VALDISERRI

Messages From the Edge:
Paigeisms for Transformational Healing

THE RED BAG

CONNECTING THE JOURNEY OF HEALING THROUGH LIFE, DEATH & BEYOND

PAIGE VALDISERRI
M.Ed. LPC, NCC, BCETS, RMT

Red Bag Press

Cover design by Emily Halbert and Sarah O'Neill
Book layout by Richard Fenwick at *Good Looking Books*
Red bag photo by Alexa Nicole McNair
Author photo by Susan Johnson
Image by Tomertu/Shutterstock.com

ISBN: 978-0-69291-701-7

I dedicate this book to my best friend, lover, cheerleader, support system and editor, my husband Tim. Your gift of writing enhanced the book tremendously with your endless hours of editing and patience with me as we relived together some of the darkest and most challenging times of our lives. Your openness in sharing with the world intimate details of your personal journey as a quest to help others is commendable and not something most men would share but need to begin to do. I am grateful for every moment we have together and I look forward to how we can continue making a positive difference in people's lives throughout the world. I love you!!

CONTENTS

FOREWORD

Chances are something pulled you in and drew your attention to this book. Perhaps it was the mysterious cover or the interesting juxtaposition of the personal and professional experiences Paige brings to the table. Or maybe you've always sensed there was something more than "Earth to Earth, Ashes to Ashes and Dust to Dust." Perhaps you want to know what the Red Bag is or exemplifies. Whatever it was that compelled you to pick up this book and begin reading, be prepared to feel a tug at your heartstrings, pride in the strength of the human spirit, and a willingness to explore and accept there are 'gifts,' interventions, and techniques outside our normal experiences. This is a wonderfully unique book filled with the gamut of emotions, teachings, and life experiences as written by one who has spent her life helping others.

Without giving too much away, let me give you my take on what to expect from the read. You'll gain an understanding of Paige's 'gifts' and how she's learned to hone them through the years to help others. You'll be exposed to the raw emotions and examples of human resilience, decency, compassion, and unity in the wake of what was once the unthinkable – the atrocity of the 9/11 attacks. You'll witness actual experiences that demonstrate the efficacy of these gifts and how they improve human effectiveness and efficiency but most of all you'll see how personal wholeness can be gained through the utilization of various healing techniques and methods.

Who is Paige Valdiserri you might ask. She is a friend, co-worker and believer that we can "do better" for others. She is passionate about the integration of alternative therapies and techniques into what is considered traditional delivery of health care services. I first met Paige in a professional capacity as I was asked to evaluate one of her teaching seminars and give my opinion of her and the message she was delivering. What I saw that day was an articulate, intelligent professional with a definite presence. She was passionate about her message, open to criticism and skepticism, but above all she was fearless. She can be a soft touch or "subtle as an ax between the eyes" as the situation requires. I have known her now for over ten years as we have collaborated on multiple projects. She has firsthand experience providing care in some of the most difficult and challenging situations such as Iraq, Africa, and Ground Zero, (New York). Her approach is individualized and in collaboration with her clients.

The introduction will give you a good idea of who Paige is and her 'gifts' and how in retrospect her work at Ground Zero helped her realize more could be done by training in multiple traditions and combining the best of those to develop her own approaches to healing. As you continue your journey through the book you will encounter Allison, a young woman who succumbed to a deadly form of breast cancer at the tender age of twenty-eight just as she completed her nursing degree. You will see how Paige's unique approach for finding meaning in the disease and her special 'gifts' helped Allison and her family through the transitioning process of death. This may have you look at death and the dying process in a very different and possibly comforting and peaceful lens.

After the Transition: A Mother's Message is one of the most heartfelt and deeply moving tributes from the parent of a deceased loved one you will ever read. Written from the heart of a mother who continues to battle the unbearable grief of losing a child, especially at such a young age and in the manner in which it happened, you will see and feel true love and compassion and will learn what it means to give permission. As you continue through you will run into Death Visited Me which describes a transition point for Paige when she came to understand that we are not alone, even in our darkest times.

Lest you think Paige or any of us are free from trauma, *Life Interrupted* brings to light one of our greatest fears - the real possibility of losing our spouse or significant other, more specifically, watching their demise as they wither both physically and mentally from the ravages of chronic illness. It is a salient reminder to all of us, including care-givers that we are not immune to life's traumas. However, it will leave you with a hopeful message of how meaning and gifts can be found in the most challenging of times. She will help inspire a re-connection to the life-giving support of nature and will offer unique perspectives on how we might approach, conceptualize, and even talk about the often-considered taboo topic of death. Her experiences will leave you wanting to know more about this and many other unexplainable facets of the human experience.

Paige will show how integrated health care can fill the gaps left when traditional or alternative therapies alone are not enough. It will be understood that wellness and wholeness is a team sport. No one methodology has all the answers and together we can all benefit. No judging, no diagnosing, no stigma – just tools to increase our capacities and keep us in the game.

Oh wait, what about that Red Bag? What does it exemplify? You will have to put your own meaning to it but let me be bold enough to give you mine. We all have our baggage, which is not all bad. We place our fears, tragedies, and our shortfalls and successes in that bag. What we often fail to see is that as we fill that bag with those experiences, we also fill the bag with the tools used to overcome our adversity. It's a bag we continually fill with more tools and the more tools we have the more likely we will have the right tool for the job. If all we have is a hammer, swatting flies can be an interesting prospect! In this, Paige has done an excellent job intertwining her mystical gifts, alternative therapies and techniques designed to allow one to become connected to their inner knowing on a deeper level. Enjoy the read as much as I did.

Kenneth L. Jones

PA-C, MPAS, Emergency Medicine, USAF Retired

Chief, Medical Operations 820th Security Forces Group (Antiterrorism/Force Protection)

INTRODUCTION

There was always something different about me. I came into this world bridging life, death and psychic realms as my mother became gravely ill and suffered a near death experience soon after my birth, leaving the responsibility of raising me during that first crucial year to her mother, my Grammy. My grandmother had the gift of psychic and clairvoyant abilities, as she was able to see an individual's past, present, and future without invitation. This 'gift,' albeit in a different form, was passed along to me and I have been learning to hone it to assist others ever since.

Having experienced trauma throughout my life, my senses became acutely attuned to the nuances of how the mind, and more importantly the body, stores, processes, and ultimately responds to traumatic events. First and foremost as a survival skill, I began to develop ways to cope and deal with traumatic events, which led me down a natural path of wanting to help others going through similar situations. This path began to manifest at a young age when I volunteered as a Candy Striper at our local hospital outside Philadelphia at age thirteen. Although there were many places throughout the hospital where we Candy Stripers worked, my pull was to the Emergency Room where I witnessed some of the most horrific, yet angelic, scenes of human existence. It was there in the ER where I began to discover my true calling and purpose here in this lifetime, which is to help others in their times of greatest need. Not only was I comfortable in the ER but I found great satisfaction and a sense of inner peace through being able to provide comfort and support to those experiencing life-changing events. And so my journey as a healer began . . .

My life would take various turns through the education field as a teacher and through corporate environments in the business arena but my heart belonged to helping those in need at their most challenging times. Although firmly entrenched and enjoying the rewards of teaching, I recognized this calling, entered a master's degree program in counseling, and would follow this up with a post-master's certification in trauma therapy. Interestingly as I was immersed in my post-master trauma studies and just beginning to establish my counseling career in private practice, the events of September 11, 2001 shook the foundations of our country, and the world for that matter. Intuitively, I knew I had to be in New York City.

I would commute to New York City from Philadelphia for a three-month period as a member of Crisis Care Network responsible for giving Critical Incident Stress Debriefings. As this event was transformational for our country and the world as a whole, need I say how transformational this experience was for me personally. While working with hundreds of people who were directly and indirectly affected by this tragedy, I began to notice the body's response to a traumatic event and its connection to an individual's physical, mental, emotional, energetic and spiritual being. This helped lay the groundwork for one of the most important aspects of my healing approach, which I believe, is recognizing the body holds life stories and is the true source of healing. I believe the power to heal ultimately comes from within each of us, thus, I see my role as being a guide, a facilitator, and a coach who is able to see the bigger spiritual picture and one who helps individuals get in touch and reconnect with their true, authentic selves. This process of empowerment means I have my clients take ownership of their bodies, and ultimately their healing, for I truly believe we must not only live but heal from the 'inside out.'

This experience at Ground Zero not only shaped how I would make it my life's journey to research, explore, and apply techniques from many different healing traditions as well as customs, but ultimately helped me create my own healing approach. This integrative approach addresses the physical, emotional, energetic, medical, mental, nutritional and spiritual components of wellness. I would train and become certified in several research-backed techniques and theories such as Cognitive behavioral theory (CBT), EMDR, Emotional Freedom Technique (EFT), and Subconscious Restructuring. I would also become certified and integrate many modalities and healing strategies from non-Western traditions and models such as Kundalini yoga, various forms of energy medicine, Reiki, Biodynamic Craniosacral Trauma Therapy, color therapy, chakra medicine therapy, past life regression, and shamanic healing.

While I pay close attention to research-backed and evidence-based treatments, I do not disclaim or discredit the work of ancient civilizations and traditions, as well as cutting-edge modalities that address the energetic, vibrational and spiritual needs of my clients. To that point, I help my clients expand their spiritual understanding as it relates to their overall health and wellness. This is completely separate and should not be confused with whatever religious beliefs they might have prior to our work. I see my role as being able to expand their understanding as opposed to advocating or challenging any particular religious belief. I do believe having a strong faith-base is very important and my work is all about complementing and expanding rather than challenging or changing belief systems.

Although my work at Ground Zero served as the catalyst for treating clients from a holistic perspective, there is another big piece of the healing puzzle: my intuitive and clairvoyant 'gifts.' As opposed to using them in a psychic sense, I use these gifts to help guide my clients toward finding their own inner wisdom and knowing, as well as their own mystical gifts. This helps them find deeper meaning and purpose in traumatic and life-changing events by helping them understand there is more than just this lifetime. I also use my gifts to assist them in connecting to their spiritual guides, angels, and loved ones who have transitioned as a means of support outside this earthly realm.

Subsequently to Ground Zero, my work has taken me through the halls of the Pentagon where I began as an EAP counselor for the DiLorenzo Tricare Health Clinic and would later be hired by the Pentagon Force Protection Agency (PFPA) to develop and implement holistic Employee Support Services programs for the Pentagon police force, Site R (Defense Department alternative command site) personnel, first-responder communities and their families. I would later find myself on the sands of Iraq as the Director of Behavioral Health for an international workforce medical services company where I designed holistic behavioral health programs for government, military, first responders, medical, local national linguists and contracted personnel. In addition, I would also have the opportunity to travel to the war-ravaged country of Rwanda where I worked with local officials as part of an international People-to-People delegation to address PTSD and systemic solutions for victims of the genocide.

Over the last two decades I've had the honor of assisting individuals in private practice, disaster response and emergency preparedness, international medical operations and critical incident stress debriefings, to help them go from a place of personal "fracturing" to a state of wholeness. I am forever indebted to the trust and faith they have put in me and it is for this that I feel the time is right to share my insight with a larger audience through this book. I expect to be challenged, as I have so many times throughout my career, particularly from individuals from organizations unwilling to look or think 'outside the box' when it comes to integrating non-Western approaches but the results of the work I have done speaks for itself. I know I may be met with skepticism and possibly outright disbelief but I urge even those who are the most cynical to keep an open mind as I take you through this journey.

Through the many people I have met along my journey who are connected to their mystical gifts, including many clients who have had Near Death Experiences, and the personal experiences I have had receiving messages from beyond this earthly realm, I began to see a larger theme playing out. Whether the messages came through dreams, loved ones who had transitioned, traumatic events, the land and its animals, or some other form, we could sense something bigger than ourselves, something more advanced than our human form, trying to contact us and give us vital information to help us process, understand and give meaning to our existence, as well as help us cope with the challenges we face living this earthly existence.

Throughout my life, I have been fortunate to have my angels, my spiritual guides, and the Divine travel with me every step of the way. Even in my darkest times, they were there to support me on my journey. If you look back over your own life, I bet you, too, have had those who have stepped in just at the right time with a much-needed message and/or support. Make no mistake, these individuals never show up by coincidence, by fluke, by chance, or by luck, but rather by poignant design in the greater scheme of things. Perhaps there is a bigger force, a vibration, or an energy out there connecting us all and binding us together in ways we have yet to imagine. And perhaps life's most challenging events and traumatic experiences serve to make us aware and bring us back to the divine knowledge that we truly are not alone. I invite you not to fear these messages and gifts but rather invite them in and connect with the knowledge, insight and support they provide.

The stories and experiences throughout this book will touch you, challenge you, and possibly transform the way you look at the world, and most of all they will give you hope during the darkest and most challenging of times. I know my intuitive gifts and the beliefs I will share about death and the afterlife may be met with uncertainty, but my hope is that each of you reading this book will look at what I have to say and the experiences I've had both personally and professionally as a way of expanding, rather than replacing or changing, your current belief systems. This is my personal wish for all of you as you embark on your own personal healing journeys.

The Red Bag

Connecting the Journey of Healing through Life, Death & Beyond

*"Find the invisible within the visible,
the gift within the trauma,
and the message in the challenge."*

~ Paige Valdiserri

1

THE GIFT IS PASSED

Everyone's birth occurs divinely no matter the imperfect conditions and outcomes. It is always at the right time, in the right place, and for specific reasons. My birth and the first year of my life was no different except for the fact that I was straddling psychic realms, illness and death.

I was born October 19, 1965 in Bryn Mawr Pennsylvania. My mother, who was thirty-two at the time, began experiencing odd bodily symptoms shortly after my birth. My mom would describe her body being taken over by a feeling of "spinning out into space," almost like a tornado taking her "further away into the heavens," which made her extremely dizzy and disoriented. Her tone of voice changed to the point where it sounded as if she was yelling when trying to communicate, something my father had to consistently point out and tell her to tone down. She also felt an overall sense of fatigue throughout the day but attributed this to the combination of just having given birth, moving into a new home, and feeling the need to push herself to prepare for the upcoming holidays.

Up until this point, my mom's body had slowly been giving her messages and clues that something in her body needed attention. By the time Christmas came around, her previous symptoms were occurring more consistently with new ones surfacing as well. She began having difficulty remembering simple tasks around the house. In addition, her eyes began developing a film over them making it challenging to see. Somewhere around this time she went to see our family doctor and was diagnosed with nephritis – an inflammation of the kidneys. He believed it had been brought on by strep throat so she was prescribed heavy doses of penicillin coupled with bed rest and was told it might become terminal if improvement didn't occur within three months. Even though she followed the doctor's orders, after a month her symptoms continued to worsen. By this time her memory began failing as she recalled to me not being able to remember the days of the week, month, or year during this time. Her hair and nails had stopped growing and all she was able to do was lay in bed and sleep. My mom had become disconnected to her body and the daily living of life.

Not being able to care for me, her new baby, was beyond frustrating. She knew my dad couldn't work, take care of an infant and my brother and sister, so my grandmother, my mom's mother, came to live with us. Grammy was not like other grandmothers, or most people for that matter. She had the unusual gift of being able to see a person's past, present, and future by reading tea leaves or using a regular deck of playing cards without having them reveal any information about themselves. She was a strong-willed, opinionated, and vivacious woman with a warm personality that was infectious. She was born in Scotland in 1898 and as a young girl would give tea leaf readings for the commoners in the village where she lived; never thinking this was a unique gift but rather just something she could do like anyone else. She would break apart a regular teabag in a cup and add a little bit of warm water. She would then have the person drink the water which in turn would allow the tea leaves to form around the cup providing her with information about the person. Her unique talent was utilized throughout the village as word of my grandmother's gift began to spread. While working in the kitchen as a cook for a family whom my grandmother referred to as royalty, she was summoned by the lady of the house for a reading. After the success of this initial reading, she was permanently moved from the kitchen to the main house where she would perform readings daily.

When World War I broke out in 1914, my grandmother, along with many other young women, would gather at homes or churches to knit stockings to send to the soldiers. The stockings were taken to a place similar to our USO where soldiers would randomly receive them. Each young woman would place their name and address in the stockings they had knitted in the hopes the soldier who received it would find them, and possibly call for them after the war had ended. After the war, a young Scottish soldier, William Gibson, who had served as a Gordon Highlander and had received a certificate of high service from the war department signed personally by Sir Winston Churchill, received one of my grandmother's stockings and showed up at her doorstep to begin a courtship that would lead to an immigration to America.

My grandfather had set his sights on the United States and began the process for the two of them to immigrate. In 1924, my grandfather left for America leaving my grandmother behind so he could find work as a metallurgical engineer and create a foundation before he sent for her. A year later in May of 1925, my grandmother left Scotland and began the journey to America through Ellis Island, New York. For the trip, she took two wedding dresses, a marzipan cake, and my grandfather's full kilt dress uniform he wore in the war. As she entered Ellis Island and was confronted by the immigration officer asking for her papers, the officer spotted my grandfather's full kilt dress uniform. Even though her papers were in order to enter the country, the officer told her that he would only grant her entrance if she gave him the dress uniform. She had no recourse but to hand it over. She would, however, reunite with my grandfather and they would end up getting married on May 18, 1925 in 'The Little Church Around the Corner,' which today is called the Church of the Transfiguration in New York City.

Once my grandparents settled in Donora, Pennsylvania, my grandmother began giving readings out of their home. In time, word began to spread about her unique gift all the way up to Hollywood royalty where stars such as Ingrid Berman and Elizabeth Taylor became part of her clientele. At one point she was even approached by a Hollywood producer, whose wife had been close to my grandmother, about moving to California where he would help her start her own business. Although my Grammy was very excited for this opportunity as she had an adventurous spirit and a zeal for living life to the fullest, my grandfather was a quiet, reserved man who enjoyed living a simple life away from the limelight. The move never happened.

A year before my birth, my grandfather died of a heart attack leaving my mother and my grandmother reeling with grief. When I came into the picture a year later, my grandmother would find herself straddling many realms as she was still grieving the death of her husband while being asked to care for an infant whose mother was inching closer to death every day. I was born into the grieving of my grandfather, the illness and potential death of my mother, and the psychic realms and gifts of my grandmother.

These were the energies that greeted me and surrounded me when I was new to this world – a Grandmother who straddled the worlds with her psychic gifts and a Mother who was straddling the worlds of life and death without understanding exactly what she was experiencing or why. Although my mother was bedridden and incapable of taking care of me, my Grammy would continue to lay me on my mother's chest several times a day so a connection could be made between the two of us. During this time my mother would ask herself and God why this was happening to her. As the illness progressed, so did her fear of not being able to see her children grow up. She would often share these fears with my father, who in turn, planted a tree outside of her window so she could see the change of seasons. He would tell her again and again that he would not let her go as there were many more years left in their journey together as a married couple – a journey that has lasted until the time of this writing.

As my first birthday approached, my mother, still bedridden, would experience a chilling near death experience (NDE). She was awakened one morning by what appeared to be a large black curtain heading directly for her from across her bedroom. She told me it felt like a gigantic black storm pushing the curtain from her right side with the intent of moving it to her far left. She knew at that moment she was going to die. She had little time before the curtain of death would encompass her as she could feel herself floating above her physical body. She heard herself saying, "Please God, allow me time to put my house in order" as the thought of leaving her husband behind with two small children and an infant was too much to bear. At that moment, an angel arrived in flowing robes, her hair light, and her face clear and ethereal and radiating brilliantly like a floodlight.

As she pushed back the curtain, it began to change colors from black to white. Her presence emanated a deep love and caring for my mom. The angel spoke to her telling her it was not her time to go as she had much living left to do in this lifetime. She would once again be able to raise her children. At this moment during her near death experience, she realized she was not going to die but my grandmother and my father still had yet to realize this. My mother, who was floating above her physical body, could see both of them crying by her bedside. She first tried to speak then resorted to shouting to tell them that she was going to live but not even a whisper could come out of her mouth. Suddenly, she was pulled back into her physical body where she felt a tremendous sense of relief and was now able to speak and communicate with my dad and my grandmother about all that had just occurred and the messages she was given.

The next day my mother knew she was headed in the direction of healing and was getting a new lease on life but there were lessons she had learned and messages she had been given through this experience that she needed to take in and process. For one, she realized "life could be taken away at any moment." She learned the caregiver's role can often times be harder than the patient's as they must shoulder the burden of the responsibilities and can be left with a helpless feeling for not being able to 'fix' the situation. She also found, to use her own words, "it was easy to accept all the good things life had to offer but it was more important to learn to accept the part of life that caused pain." While interviewing my mother for this chapter, she had what many would describe as an "a-ha moment." As she was reliving her illness and near death experience, she said to me, "I think you were the one who brought me back Paige" when she realized her NDE coincided with my first birthday. When I heard this, I knew in that moment she was right as every fiber and cell in my body resonated with her words.

As my mother shared the experience of her NDE and the description of the angel who appeared to help her, chills ran through my body. This angel who showed up fifty years ago for my mother is the same angel who has been working side-by-side with me when I am working with my medically ill clients. The same identifiers my mother used to describe her – the flowing robes, light hair, clear and ethereal face – are exactly how I would describe the angel who has been working with me. Just as she pulled back the curtain of death from a place of deep love and caring for my mom, she, too, emanates a warmth, comfort, and peace that assists me with my clients' treatment.

Nine months after I interviewed my mother for this chapter, she was rushed to the hospital with what appeared to be a stroke. Although a spot was found on her brain, it proved to be inconclusive. While she was in the hospital I spoke with her several times to check-in and see how she was doing. It was hard for me to make sense of what she was saying as her speech was disconnected and so was her train of thought. What I intuitively felt was that even though my mother was trying to speak in her human form, she was splitting away from her physical body and trying to communicate on a soul level. It felt to me like she was experiencing something similar to the near death experience she had when I was born where she was once again straddling life and death.

A few days later after she had been released from the hospital, she shared with me something that had been scaring her. She told me about a voice from the afterlife that had been speaking to her while at the same time organ music was playing in the background. This voice stated it was here to take her from this lifetime. She told the voice to leave her alone as she didn't want to go with it. Upon hearing this I gave her my perspective and understanding that this was a voice reaching out to her from beyond to communicate about the dying process. It didn't necessarily mean death was at her doorstep but it did mean the process of getting her prepared for her eventual transition could be underway. I told her ignoring this voice would not be a wise choice as it would only get stronger and might hasten the dying process. We discussed verbiage she could use to communicate with the voice to better understand the true meaning behind the visit. I gently reminded her of the NDE she had experienced after my birth and how she had been given a loving preview of how the soul never dies. Interestingly enough, my mother commented that while I was speaking with her about ways to communicate with this voice, both the voice and the organ music had gone silent. It was as if this voice knew I understood the process that was taking place.

Two days later I called to wish my mother a happy 84th birthday. During our conversation she shared a message she had been given the day before. The evening before her birthday, she told my dad she felt that she was going to die that night. She removed all of her jewelry, placed it in her jewelry box, and gave my dad the money she had saved before they went to sleep. You can imagine how anxious they both were for different reasons. Sometime in the middle of the night, she heard the voice but this time the message was very different. The voice stated it would not be her time yet and that she would get better – a message synonymous with the one she had been given around my first birthday. My mother had once again been straddling illness, death and messages from beyond, but this time, I was there to give her the insight into the voice which was passed down to me from her mother.

As for my grandmother, she would become a very strong influence in my life as we spent much time together through the years. As a young girl, I remember her living with us on and off and often being my built-in babysitter. Late at night I would creep into her bedroom, wake her up, and lay at the foot of her bed as we talked the night away. We would play dress-up together, act out plays, make cakes in my EZ Bake Oven and for hours upon hours she would watch me perform commercials using my mom's cleaning products. You can imagine how upset my mother was each time she would find empty bottles of cleaners. She was my cheerleader and my number one fan. More times than I can count, she would sit me in front of the tea leaves and ask me to read what I saw as she consistently told me I had a gift. I would humor her by agreeing but I really didn't believe what she was telling me was true. However, she did have a knowing about me and my gifts. Although I didn't have my grandmother's gift of reading tea leaves, I did have other gifts that would come into focus and develop over time.

Grammy would end up living to be 100 years old. The evening after her funeral services, I returned to my apartment alone and placed her picture next to my bedside telling her she would always be with me. In the middle of the night, I was abruptly awakened by a very bright light. As I sat up and peered down to the foot of my bed, there she was standing in full color letting me know that she would always be with me, too.

Writing this chapter and seeing the experiences laid out in front of me has given me a greater appreciation for the bigger picture of how my journey in this lifetime is to help others and how the circumstances surrounding my birth have led to this. I believe on a soul level, my mother had a knowing about the purpose of my journey as she named me Paige. Although she named me this because I was the last chapter in her book of children, the actual meaning of the name means 'to serve.' I was born into this world straddling two divine feminine energies: one was my Grammy's which was about naturally embracing psychic gifts and the other was my mother's which was about struggling through illness and walking the road of death. These energies enveloped me and gave me the foundation for being able to help people on their path by bridging life, death, illness, trauma, mystical gifts, and messages from beyond. The experiences around my birth and throughout my life have allowed me to be the bridge from this world to others, from human form to soul, from life to death, and everything in between.

2

THE RED BAG

The morning the planes hit the Twin Towers, a feeling of 'pang' came over me as I opened the refrigerator where I had been living in the outskirts of Philadelphia. I wasn't sure what the pang meant, but I knew it wasn't good. A few minutes later the confusion of the first plane's crash into the Twin Towers hit the news. It was first reported as an accident but deep in my gut I knew otherwise. Minutes later as the second plane hit the other Tower, our nation's deepest fears were confirmed — we were under attack.

I began urgently calling my friends and loved ones as I drove to Delaware, where I worked as a trauma therapist. Were they safe? Were their families safe?

When I walked into work, I was hit by the chaotic buzz of fear, panic, and sheer disbelief. The need to connect with loved ones was paramount. Once in my office, I began receiving strong messages from deep within: *You need to be in New York. It is your time. We've been preparing you for this.* I had been receiving intuitive messages like these throughout my whole life. Sometimes they come in the form of dreams, visualizations, a sense of what will happen and clear messages that come through my heart center. Throughout my lifetime I have learned to recognize, listen and trust them, no matter how different or off the beaten path, they may have seemed.

They always come from a place of my higher knowing and for my highest good and purpose.

At this point I needed to step outside to get some air. I walked outside of the practice and stood alone on the grass looking up at the sky when I felt a strange pushing motion hitting the back of my heels. I can tell you without a doubt there was no one standing anywhere near me but I kept feeling a sensation as if someone was standing behind me tapping the back of my heels with a foot. As I kept looking back, there was no human in sight. With each tap on my heels, the messages kept coming to me: *Don't stand still. Move forward. Do what you need to do to get to Ground Zero.* The heel-kicking kept continuing until I finally relented and listened wholeheartedly to the messages I was being given. I knew I had to go to New York.

These messages were validated by other senior therapists in the practice, especially my mentor, Margie, who felt the same way about my need to go. I had lived, trained and worked with trauma most of my life. It felt second nature to me, so I knew in my gut, Ground Zero was where I needed to be. Although I had a full caseload of clients in Delaware, Margie and the senior therapists understood this need to go and we made it happen. For the next three months, I would commute to New York City during the week for several days at a time as a member of Crisis Care Network to help the healing process begin for those devastated by this tragedy.

For a trip like this, since I had yet to own a suitcase with wheels, my red gym bag, which was more akin to a duffel bag than a suitcase, was the only piece of luggage that would work. When my sister dropped me off at 30th Street Station in Philly, I had no idea how this red bag would transform my life and what it would come to symbolize. Not only did it carry my clothes, toiletries and amenities necessary for the journey, but it also carried my soul's purpose. It would come to represent the collective experience of all the hope, fear, pain, and loss I would hear from the countless stories of those directly and indirectly affected by this tragedy. It would serve as a repository for all the emotions I would hear from others, as well as become a container for all the emotions I had to process while I did my best to do what therapists do and that is to hold the space for others. Most importantly, because of the mysterious nature in which the red bag was handled, as you will soon read, it would become a message and a sign that I was not operating in this experience, or this lifetime for that matter, by myself. As you will see, I was clearly and undeniably not alone on this journey.

A week later as I prepared for the first of many trips to New York, I remember being overcome by a deep sense of quiet and a feeling that I was being connected to something much larger than myself. As I sat waiting for the train to arrive in 30th Street Station, I felt a sense of excitement as I knew deep in the fibers of my soul this work would tap into my purpose here in this world but I also felt a great level of apprehension and trepidation as I was about to venture into something with a magnitude that neither I nor our entire country had ever experienced. When the train finally arrived, as I reached down to pick up my red bag a gentleman appeared asking if he could carry it for me. Ever since the terrorist attack it seemed as if a wave of compassion had spread throughout the country, which made offers like this seem normal and nothing out of the ordinary. I, of course, accepted the offer and he carried my bag all the way down the steps to the train until I was able to find my seat.

When I arrived a few hours later at Penn Station in New York City, before I had a chance to get off of the train, I was approached by another man who offered to carry my red bag. Once again, I gladly accepted. He carried it from the train to a block beyond the station at which point he placed the bag on the ground and apologized for not being able to carry it further for me as he was going in an opposite direction. I thanked him profusely for his kindness and smiled as I watched him walk away. Not only was I grateful for the help but I enjoyed the conversations I had been able to strike up with both of these men as they both had asked what I was traveling to New York for. Since I still had a few blocks to go, I reached down for my bag but before I had a chance to pick it up, a third gentleman arrived on the scene offering to carry it yet again. By this point, I began to know these encounters were not coincidental. These weren't just random acts of kindness or chivalry.

Once again, I accepted the offer and he carried my bag several blocks to the lobby of the hotel where I was staying. Just like the previous gentleman, I thanked him and he wished me luck as we parted ways. While checking into the hotel, the bell hop already had my red bag in hand before I could reach for it. Once I got upstairs to my room and began to look out onto the city, the thought occurred to me that not once did I have to carry my red bag during this entire trip. Could this have been the Divine or a Divine Source stepping in knowing I would have more than enough to carry in the next three months? Only time would tell.

Before I began my work at Ground Zero, I had a chance to survey the scene with a friend of mine from New Jersey who had been assisting those whose loved ones had died in the attack with their personal death claims. On our way to Ground Zero together, I felt the heaviness, angst

and profound stillness of the city. We stopped often at
the countless living altars of candles, notes, pictures, and
pleads for any information on missing loved ones. These
had sprung up throughout the city as a heartbreaking reminder of the pain, toll, and desperation that gripped the
city. I assumed Ground Zero would be loud with movement. Instead it was filled with an eerie silence. I remember
looking at the remains of the structure, searching for spaces
where air could possibly get through in hopes that someone could still be alive. I, too, wanted and needed to believe
that life underneath the rubble was still hopeful.

As we took in the hard work of the first responders, a
team of eight fatigued firefighters emerged from the rubble.
They were surrounded on either side by teams of onlookers,
many of whom were clinging to the hope that their loved
ones would be found alive. Sadly, it became clear that no
such signs were to be found and that they were simply walking back to their firehouses for a long overdue break. As
they moved through the tunnel of people, you could hear a
pin drop and then all of a sudden the quiet was pierced as
we all began to cheer, clap, cry and yell encouraging words
of love, support and gratefulness for all they were doing. I
noticed many of these men had tears streaming down their
faces and appeared hunched over, almost as if they didn't
feel worthy of the appreciation. I found myself wrapped up
in a swirl of emotion and so began the many weeks I would
be assisting the people of New York. The days ahead would
be long, intense, and fulfilling, even spiritual. It was time
to do whatever small piece I could to help the city and the
people of New York begin the healing process.

After that first day, I eagerly began my work performing
Critical Incident Stress Debriefings as a Crisis Care Network provider for various groups of people from firms on

Wall Street and the surrounding areas. This work entailed working with numerous individuals in various group settings, to process all they had experienced on the day of the attack, the weeks after and how the event was impacting their daily lives. Many of the folks I debriefed had been in direct view of the towers and had actually been able to see the planes hitting the buildings, as well as their eventual collapse. They had also seen the faces of those trapped in the buildings. I heard countless stories of how hopeless and helpless they felt while watching in horror, not knowing if anyone would be able to escape. In those moments, they would not realize the ongoing impact this attack would have on their lives.

As someone who has worked with trauma for decades, I can tell you that experiences like these lodge in the body leaving its imprint. For these folks, the impact of this attack and what they witnessed, would bleed out with nightmares, hyper-vigilance, and scenes playing over in their minds like movie clips, sleepless nights, and daily fear that another attack was inevitable. As you can imagine, the impact from these events, not only directly affected those who lost loved ones but also the first responders and therapists, such as myself, who had to battle our own vicarious traumatization from exposure to the horrors of what we were hearing, seeing, and trying to process. This is what I and many other trauma therapists were faced with on a daily basis as we functioned as the 'hidden figures' trying to shepherd those through this unfathomable event.

Throughout my three-month journey, I would have several specific incidents that would leave lasting impressions on me. One of them happened to be an experience I had on the subway. One evening after work while traveling on the subway, the fear and anxiety I had been hearing throughout the debriefings was now permeating throughout the city. I had been traveling on the subway when all of a sudden the lights went out and the train came to a screeching halt prior to our stop. You could just feel the fear and anxiety in the air. People began to cry and shout in panic. To compound the situation, our cell phones weren't able to get service. Trapped in this subterranean cage, I was able to remain calm and did my best to soothe those around me who were in complete panic but the damage had already been done. For a city reeling from the events of the attacks, this was another reminder of how vulnerable we were and served to reinforce our fears that we were under attack again. I can't tell you how long the train had stopped in that position but when the lights did come back on and the train began to move, the relief was no match for the unbridled fear. When the train arrived at the destination, people ran desperately out to get to daylight where they could begin calling someone to share what had just occurred. Sadly, this had become the new normal for New Yorkers: hypervigilance, startled responses, anxiety, lack of trust and fear of the next attack.

As the weeks and months began to pile up, it became increasingly difficult to tear myself away from Ground Zero, both mentally and physically, to serve my clients back in Delaware. It also became difficult in general to return to normal life back in Philly with friends and family. I had become so entrenched and emotionally invested in my work up in New York that I found it hard to 'switch off' and return to the normal existence I had before. This is the essence of what trauma therapists do for their clients – help them re-adjust and re-acclimate to a new normal, although this time the 'new normal' had shifted for me as well.

Each time I would return to my hotel which by now had become my second home, I was always greeted with such care, warmth and understanding. I will never forget the kindness the hotel concierge extended to me one evening after work. He had an extra ticket free of charge to the Lion King as Broadway had just reopened. He mentioned how he had seen the long hours I had been putting in taking care of others and wanted to give something back to me in return. I graciously accepted as tears filled my eyes. The Lion King movie had always been one of my favorites. As I walked the quiet streets to the theatre, the significance of the story–life, death, rebirth–hadn't yet occurred to me. From a cathartic standpoint, I sat crying throughout the entire production watching this beautiful, colorful, and poignant play. Art was imitating life – the cycle of life. And I had been smack dab in the middle of it every day.

Although it was tough to pull myself away from Ground Zero, I reached a point in mid-November when I knew it would be my last. I knew I had to pull back. As exhilarating and personally fulfilling as the work was, I reached a point of mental and physical exhaustion. Every muscle, fiber, and cell in my body was beyond depleted. I needed to take care of myself and literally had nothing left in the tank to give anyone. I had heard every unthinkable traumatic story, shared the space with others in their deepest of grief, held many in my arms as their tears flowed onto my shoulders and continually gave a higher spiritual perspective (when appropriate) of hope and understanding to a situation that felt hopeless and helpless. I had given all I had to everyone who needed me after this horrific and life-changing event. On one hand I was ready to return home but on the other hand I didn't want to leave. I equate this situation to a soldier returning home from battle because of an injury. Even though he or she is away from the danger, there is still that part of him or her that wants to remain, and feels guilty, for leaving comrades behind. I felt like this as well. Even though my heart was still in New York, I knew I had a responsibility to myself and others to ensure that my mental, physical, and emotional exhaustion didn't bleed out. It was time for me to step away and begin to recover and process all that I had experienced. That last train ride from New York to Philly would prove to be the longest.

And so my three-month journey of weekly commutes would come to an end. As I looked back, it occurred to me that I *NEVER* had to physically carry my red bag throughout the journey. Different men kept showing up to carry it for me at various times throughout the trip. I'm not sure how to explain it – in a cosmic or spiritual sense it was as if the Universe was supporting me for taking care of others. But just like the trip began, something interesting happened on the way back.

Just like my time in New York, if I wasn't busy debriefing folks in an official capacity my time was filled with informal conversations as my background and personality lent themselves to any particular situation. It was no different on the train as I could barely find any time for myself to sit quietly and try to process my experience because I had come to know the conductors so well through this three month journey, that they regularly looked forward to talking to me as they were also in need. I arrived in Philly completely wiped out and with almost no energy to make the trek home, let alone carry my red bag. As had happened week after week and month after month, like clockwork another gentleman showed up offering to carry my bag. He carried it off the train until we reached the foot of the escalator, when he realized he had forgotten something and had to leave me with it. To make matters worse, the escalator happened to be broken, which was the first time it had been broken during this entire three-month journey. So there I stood at the bottom of the broken escalator wondering how I would muster up the strength and energy to make it up.

I can't underscore the significance of that moment. It looked like the steepest, heaviest walk I would ever have to make. In the exhaustion of the moment, the emotions of the three-month journey finally hit me like a ton of bricks and I began to get very emotional. They came over me like a flood. As people walked hurriedly by me to get to the top of the steps, I just stood there with tears streaming down my face immobilized by the emotional toll this experience was taking. The broken escalator symbolized the brokenness of the people I had been helping these past months and in that moment, I, too, felt like one of the broken.

As the train emptied out and all of the folks had made their way from the platform up the broken escalator, I stood there alone staring at my red bag when something hit me. The red bag had become a metaphor for my journey. It contained the memories of everything that had happened to me these last three months from the many emotional debriefings and informal conversations I had with folks along the way to the situation on the subway and the cathartic feeling from watching the Lion King. The red bag became my placeholder for all the emotions I had carried, not only for myself but for those I carried for others. Now I stood there with nothing left to give and in desperate need of a helping hand. In that moment, I felt a hand touch mine, although this was no ordinary hand. It felt different. I can't explain it. His touch was something I had never felt before from a human hand. He gently took my hand off the strap of my bag and placed it with his, all the while smiling graciously at me without uttering a word. His presence gave me renewed strength to walk up the escalator. Together we made our way to the top as he carried my red bag, tears continuing to stream down my face.

What I remember most vividly about that experience was the feeling of being in a different time and space, perhaps a different realm. I heard nothing around us. I remember trying to say 'thank you' several times but nothing came out of my mouth. As we reached the top of the escalator, several things began to happen simultaneously. I saw the gentleman put my bag on the ground and felt him slowly put my hand back on the bag. As I felt his hand leave mine, I raised my head to try once more to say 'thank you' but just as softly and mysteriously as he'd arrived, he was gone. If you know anything about 30th Street Station in Philly, no one can disappear that quickly out of sight. Just like that, he had vanished.

As a trauma therapist, I have been 'carrying the bag' and 'holding the space' for others to work out and make sense of the events in their lives that often challenge the very core of their existence and the very purpose they see and feel for themselves in this lifetime. I have been blessed with the gift of being able to help others make sense of it all, and sometimes use my clairvoyance to help guide them to and from places they'd never expect, let alone be able to see on their own. As I have been providing these spaces for my clients and others, so, too, have others been holding the space for me. And in some cases, I firmly and unequivocally believe these others come from realms beyond this earthly existence. The experience I had with my red bag, particularly the final encounter on my last journey, was something beyond this earthly realm. It was a message from another dimension, what I have come to know is the Divine, giving me validation that I'm not alone on this journey. It was also a message that none of us are alone, even when we face the most difficult, desperate, and downright horrific challenges to our existence.

I deliver this message to you now as a placeholder of hope. No matter how bleak things seem to be, you are right where you are supposed to be at any given moment. When the mind can't wrap itself around the destruction, violence, illness, loss, and death of this lifetime, there is a support system in place for you, if you choose to be open to it that can guide you through. This doesn't mean you won't, or shouldn't for that matter, feel the emotional burden of brokenness but maybe, just maybe, you will feel and/or connect with the support that is just a whisper away . . . the Divine within us all, who may one day show up to carry your red bag.

3

DEATH VISITED ME

Long before becoming a trauma therapist, I had always been fascinated by the topic of death. Odd, you may say, but I have always had a pull to be in the middle of the action, so to speak, where the vibration of life and death flirt with each other. People have said I have a 'first responder' mentality, which would certainly make sense considering the work I have done and continue to do with the first responder population. Not only do I count them among some of my most near and dear clients but through the years I have gone on ride-alongs with police officers, cross-trained with S.W.A.T. teams, and even tried my luck participating at 'live burns' with the Arlington County (Virginia) fire department.

I can trace this penchant for action and curiosity about death back to my early childhood. When I was little I would read books and watch TV shows and movies with the most devastating and traumatic ordeals. It felt natural for me, almost as if I were hard-wired for this work. When I was thirteen, I volunteered as a Candy Striper at our local hospital. For me, I wanted to be around what I was most comfortable with and that was helping others while they were immersed in crisis, illness, pain, and possibly facing death, thus my first choice was the emergency room. I already knew and felt people coming into the ER were scared, confused, and frequently in pain so I would 'hold the space' for them by holding their hands, offering a soothing touch and helping to calm them down. Although I ended up volunteering throughout the hospital in other places, the Emergency Room was my calling and probably one of the places that sowed my seeds as a trauma therapist.

Through the years I often found myself asking God, the Universe, the angels, and the spirit world to show and teach me more about death. Intuitively I knew deep inside the more I knew and understood about death the more it would help me assist others during their darkest, saddest, and scariest times. I remember a question that came to me one morning in late August 2001 while I was in the middle of a parking lot: Are we alone when we die, even if this could be the most terrifying or violent time in our lives? Questions like this would often come up for me as my soul knew I was preparing for the next part of my journey. Sure enough, two weeks later, two planes crashed into the Twin Towers and so would come the answers to my question.

During my second trip back to New York, Crisis Care Network informed me that representatives from TD Water-house had specifically requested for me to return to continue working with their employees. I felt good about the trust I had gained and prepared myself for another intense day of hearing and processing stories of pain, fear, grief, loss and anxiety. After work that day, I returned to the same hotel, which became my second home for the next three months, and looked forward to a good night's sleep. Although this work was beyond draining, I felt a sense of peace about being able to assist others through this unspeakable nightmare. This peaceful feeling would soon be shattered.

As I lay asleep curled up in the fetal position, a strange sensation of a Presence came over me and woke me up.

Even with my eyes closed, I felt the Presence growing stronger and moving closer to my bedside until it was standing over me. Fear overwhelmed me as I could feel the sweat beginning to pour down my face to my chest. I had never felt such darkness looming over me like this. Slowly I cracked my eyes open so I could peer at bed level, never moving my head to look up. As I did this, I could make out a dark brown satchel at eye level appearing to be dangling from someone's body. It looked like a bag that had traveled many lifetimes, like the bag Indiana Jones's character carried in the Steven Spielberg movies. I didn't dare touch it or open it. The rest of the night, I lay in bed, sweating and fearful not to make any kind of movement as I was much too afraid to meet eyes with this Presence.

After what felt like a lifetime, morning finally came. The Presence and the satchel attached to it had physically disappeared. Yet as I slowly climbed out of bed and walked to the bathroom, the thickness of the Presence filled me so deeply that I couldn't shake it – get rid of it. It was now traveling inside of me and I knew it wasn't going to leave. I looked in the mirror at the bags under my eyes, which instantly filled with tears. I asked myself how in the world was I going to make it through the day. And would those I help be able to feel the cloak of heaviness that now engulfed me? I knew this Presence would accompany me and hang on me like a backpack full of bricks. I also knew I wouldn't be able to take it off.

That day at work as I was in the middle of hearing some of the most painful, traumatic, and devastating stories about the terrorist attacks, I began to receive messages from this Presence: *You need to face me to understand me. I am here for a purpose.* As the day turned into night, the dread of suffering another sleepless, sweaty, and fearful night swept over me. As I lay in bed in the same fetal position, I could feel the Presence yet again. I saw the satchel at eye level but was too afraid to move or look up. It was almost as if I felt I would die if I had to face it.

The next day was the same as the previous as I woke up feeling filled with a cloak of darkness. And just like the day before, I received messages from the Presence but this time they were louder and more intense: YOU NEED TO FACE ME TO UNDERSTAND ME. I AM HERE FOR A PURPOSE. As a trauma therapist, I thought it must be the transference of hearing all of the traumatic stories but I would soon find out this would not be the case.

That night while getting ready for bed, I knew I couldn't keep up the pace of working such long, emotional hours without sleeping. I knew I needed to surpass my fear and step into what had been visiting me. This Presence had a message and I needed to hear it.

Once again, for the third night in a row, as I settled into my fetal position under the covers, the Presence returned, except this time I felt a different energy. This time I felt a patience and could sense a feeling of guidance from it. I could feel it was here to teach me. At one point it occurred to me the question I had thrown out to the universe two weeks prior to 9-11 about dying alone in violent or terrifying moments. As the Presence moved closer I felt as if I could almost touch the dark brown satchel. I knew it was time to face this.

As I steadied myself with enough courage to look up, I saw what appeared to be a tall, thin male figure in tattered brownish grey clothing. My eyes made their way up this figure to a long, rough, thick pointy beard. Sheer panic set in as my eyes met his – they were deep, dark, and longing. I could see right through them. I felt no separation between us. I was now one with this Presence. As the panic subsided, a multitude of emotions ran through my entire being. I quickly realized these emotions were given to me by the Presence so that I could experience what many had gone through right before, during, and after death from their physical bodies. I was now getting insight into another component of death. Words couldn't describe all that was being divinely passed to me to help others through my work. I considered this gift an honor, and one that I would respect and use to help those in great need.

During 9/11, many watched in horror as people were forced to decide whether to jump from the Towers or burn to death. Many believed, including myself, that there was sheer fear, panic and pain in this type of death. However, this Presence now passed to me a different picture that cannot be seen by the human eye of what occurs when one is facing a traumatic death. It showed me that no one is alone in these dark, traumatic instances. Traveling with them and by their sides are their angels, soul families, guides and those who've transitioned before them and that there is an unconditional feeling of pure love and support that outweighs any pain, fear or panic one may be experiencing. As these emotions flooded through me, I could sense how individuals felt with the imminence of their own death. I was struck by the old saying, "Death comes knocking on your door." This didn't feel like knocking to me. It felt more like a flow, an energy, or a vibration. As I lay in bed, the pain, destruction, fear, angst, anxiety, loss and sadness I was experiencing through others had a different feeling and meaning for me now.

I had been given a gift of understanding a little about something we search to understand in this lifetime, especially when our loved ones die so traumatically. It was revealed to me that death was a natural knowing, like breathing. We already know how to do it, no matter the manner in which we transition from our physical body.

The knowledge infused within me about death by this Presence, would not only help the people I worked with at Ground Zero but would change the way I worked with people forever. That night I embraced in every fiber of my physical, mental, emotional and spiritual self: Death. This experience would now be packed into my red bag to take with me to assist others in this lifetime.

By the next morning, I was looking forward to using this knowledge to help those I was working with. This time as I walked to the bathroom and got ready for the day, I wore this cloak of death in a much different manner. It was interwoven through my whole being down to a cellular level. There was no more he and me; only us. And 'us' would travel together, always.

4

THE LIFE OF DEATH

As I lay on the table, I could feel the presence of my guides and helpers approaching for the journey. I would once again travel outside this earthly existence and be given yet another opportunity not only to expand my gifts but to bring back knowledge about a particular topic that fascinates us but one we also fear and rarely speak about – death.

Ever since I was a little girl, I have been fascinated with the concept of death. It is what pulled me to the ER as a Candy Striper and what has pulled me to work with victims of trauma, particularly victims of some of the most horrific events people experience. Having worked on scene on natural disasters and terrorist attacks and in war zones (Iraq) and war-torn villages in Africa, as well as with clients who have had to deal with suicide and terminal illness, I have been privy to many facets of death. As strange as this may seem, I've always wanted to know what it feels like to die. Is there fear? What happens to us after the transition from death? Questions like these come to me from my inner knowing. It's hard to explain but when they come, it usually means I'm going to need it in the near future to assist with those I'm working with. This insight would come soon enough.

Throughout my life, people have shown up to assist for many reasons and this time was no different. My mentor

Phyl, crossed my path when I was looking for healing practitioners who could help my husband here in Tucson. Phyl has lived her life similar to mine as we have worked in the mainstream while simultaneously utilizing our gifts. Few people understand the depth and breadth of the work I do but Phyl not only understood this, she was there to help me expand my gifts even more. Phyl is a clairvoyant/medium whose gifts were passed down from both her grandparents. Her paternal grandmother was a Choctaw Indian shaman who white people would go to after dark for healing and her Caucasian maternal grandmother had the gift of clairvoyance. Like me, Phyl is surrounded by guides and helpers beyond this earthly realm and is able to journey outside of this human existence. A few days after these questions of death came to me I ended up in her office so she could support me on this intense journey. When I arrived she intuitively knew I was coming in to investigate death. As I lay on the table with her hands on me, I could feel the presence of my guides and helpers approaching for the journey.

Before I describe this particular journey, I'd like to acknowledge at the outset this concept of journeying might be challenging for some of my readers to embrace, especially if you are trying to wrap your head around a concept that comes from an inner knowing. As human beings, many of us often place trust in aspects of religious and spiritual faiths that defy the laws of science and explanation. Journeying, too, must be taken with an article of faith as it is a concept that has many connotations and can be interpreted differently from various cultural perspectives. For me, journeying means traveling outside my physical body in my spirit/soul form upward to and through various realms outside of this world. Although this might sound strange, this ability fits within the gifts passed down to me from my grandmother in the same way Phyl's gifts were passed down to her. I am able to travel to realms where time and space are comprised very differently. The further up I've traveled, the higher the frequency and the thinner and lighter I've become until eventually I enter realms based on vibration. [*I should mention I use the terms spirit and soul interchangeably as I believe they are one in the same.]

At this point, some of you might ask if this concept is dangerous. How do I know if my spirit will return? The purpose of this specific type of journeying is to find answers to questions that come up from an inner knowing within my soul so as to bring back insightful information for my clients. Along with my educational degrees and certifications, I integrate my mystical gifts, which includes journeying, as a way to assist others, especially during their most challenging of times. But with this specific type of journey the spirit must leave the physical body and travel to realms outside of this earthly existence. Since I believe our spirit is our true self and knows the purpose of its journey, I have never had a fear of not returning to my physical body. However, along with this gift comes great responsibility and the recognition to know when journeying alone would not be wise, therefore, I knew I would need assistance from Phyl.

In this particular journey, I would be traveling with a guide whom I had never met who was thin, stern, and very serious. He would be leading me to a place I had seen before on previous journeys but had not been allowed to visit. I was excited to have permission to step into what had pulled me several times before. Typically during journeying I move quickly but this time my guide purposefully slowed me down to what felt like a 'slow-motion' speed. I had no control over my movement and my speech was also in slow-motion. As I tried to speak to Phyl, the speed of my speech matched the pace of my movements.

As my guide led me to our first stop I was shown what appeared to be a book entitled 'My Deaths.' As the name implies, this book contained images of the many ways I had died from past lifetimes. What I found interesting was that when I viewed my past deaths, which were many, I was literally emotionless. One would think it would bring up all sorts of emotions but it didn't. It was completely matter-of-fact. There were no regrets, anger, anguish, sadness . . . nothing . . . it just was. As the book closed, we moved on to the next stage of the journey.

I remember passing what in human terms looked like a classroom where some type of learning was taking place regarding death. I knew I had already learned this lesson, which my guide validated, so we moved on to the next classroom designed specifically for me. This classroom contained insight into some of the questions I had asked about death. I was shown different scenarios of what happens when violent deaths such as car accidents, bombings, fire, and violence consume a human person. What I saw and came to learn was that when a death like this occurs, there is a quick 'pulling out' – a separation from the physical body where no emotion is felt whereas deaths that are not violent, the soul gently releases from the physical body. Since our physical bodies are nothing more than the home where the soul is housed temporarily, our true essence, which is our soul, does not feel the pain, suffering and emotions associated with the violent death. Therefore, when the soul leaves the body, it also leaves behind the emotions and feelings that are found and lodged in the human form. I share this insight with you as I have often found those left behind who've had to deal with processing a violent death of their loved one, typically believe they were alone in their pain, suffering and desperation. However, what I experienced tells a much different story. Hopefully this insight will bring a measure of peace to those who have lost loved ones in such a way as we all want to know they were free from suffering in the dying process and were supported in love – my journey validated this.

After I was given insight into this separation of soul-physical body, I was then given the opportunity to experience what this separation and the dying process feels like. As I lay flat on my back, I felt a wave of energy come from my right side. It felt almost like a magnet was gently lifting my inner self away from my physical body. It moved from top to bottom and side to side in one fell swoop. It felt like the bigger loving presence of the Divine, the source that lives and breathes throughout the universe, was gently and lovingly ushering me out of the physical body. As this was happening, I felt myself begin to pant gently in small, short breaths. My breath became shallower as I was lifted up toward an opening to the upper right hand side. I could feel my body getting cooler and my fingers and toes becoming stiffer. I was able to feel my soul floating above yet simultaneously being very aware of what was happening in my physical body. It gave me the chance to experience what it was like to be in two places at one time. As my breath became shallower and the separation became greater, just like that I was instantly pulled back into my physical body. My soul had returned and it was now housed within this human vessel of my body. As I slowly opened my eyes, Phyl was at my feet holding them down to keep me as grounded as possible. It took me a little while to fully re-integrate to the point where my soul and physical body felt fully merged. My breath hadn't returned completely and the feel of my skin was not yet back to human touch.

When I finally felt like I had reintegrated, it was clear to me this journey had affected me differently than any of the others I had been on. It is hard to put into words but I felt the experience down to my core. It's not every day one leaves his or her physical body to experience the dying process and returns. It would take me several weeks to take in what had just occurred and all I had experienced. I remember feeling a sort of malaise in my body and 'self' about returning because the feeling of being without the physical body was pure joy and lightness. However, I now had new insight about the dying process I could use to assist my clients who wanted and needed to understand what their loved ones had gone through.

Death has a life of its own. It dances around us, in us, and with us before it eventually takes us. Although an inevitable occurrence in the life cycle of every living creature, death is an unknown that is often feared and avoided. As I've been peeling away the layers of the onion around death through my journeys and in my profession, I feel there is a great need to shift the way we talk about and conceptualize it. What if we began to normalize death by not being afraid to talk about it, especially when it comes to medical illness? What if it didn't seem morbid, but rather natural, to share and talk about the way we talk about life? I've found when I bring up the subject or the possibility of death with a client, a hidden release valve is opened up relieving pent-up pressure as it gives them the space and freedom to talk about what others around them can't or won't. This may mean investigating your personal beliefs about death. How did you come to them? Or did they come to you? Were they passed down to you from religious or spiritual organizations? Books? Generations of life experiences? An innate knowing? I am inviting you to get in touch with your relationship with death in a new and gentle way.

Talking about and normalizing death helps in the process of living, both before and after someone dies. Many times throughout my career I've heard over and over how my clients wish they would have had some conversations with specific questions around death, prior to their loved one's transition. What I have found is that if you and your loved one have had such conversations prior to an impending illness or sudden death, it will lessen or soften the impact of the situation. For instance, this could entail discussing various scenarios regarding the dying process such as how they would like to be remembered, the type of funeral service or celebration of life, and how they would like their physical remains to be prepared. From my experience, many of my clients would have wanted to know what their loved one wanted for them after they died as it could provide comfort and peace by releasing any guilt associated with choices made on how to live one's life after the significant other has transitioned. Going one step further, if you believe in the afterlife and the concept of the soul never dying, you might want to ask your loved one how he or she plans on communicating with you after they've transitioned. When someone we love dies, we ache to touch them, hear them, hold them one last time or know that they are okay and are somehow around us. Would it be through a song, animal, person, touch or some other fashion that would give a clear message that their soul is still around you? I have seen that having discussions like these while you are healthy or during a terminal illness can provide a measure of comfort and a sense of peace during difficult times.

Many of us carry in our red bag the fear, sadness, mystery and memories of the many ways death has shown up in our lives. Our bag holds for us the spiritual, religious, and mystical beliefs, as well as those messages given to us from beyond. Although we will never know all the aspects around the dying process and the afterlife, what I believe and have been shown, is that we only die from the physical form and the essence of our soul continues on as we are all a piece of the universal life force.

5

ALLISON'S WINGS

I was painting in my office one Sunday afternoon in the summer of 2016 when I felt a presence move through my whole physical body like the wind. This spirit felt big and expansive but also light and joyous as if it was a part of many universes and many realms all at once. As I paused from my painting, I could feel her. I knew this spirit. It was the spirit of a precious soul I had recently helped transition from a devastating battle with cancer. It was Allison.

Allison Ryan was referred to me from a client of mine in the summer of 2015 while she was battling an aggressive form of triple negative breast cancer. At the time she had gone through long bouts of chemotherapy, radiation and was beginning new clinical trials. Her illness was so aggressive it would continue to mutate and never go into remission. Although she wasn't exactly sure why she was coming to see me or how I could help, deep down on a soulful level she had a 'knowing' that she needed to be with me.

Allison was a bright, beautiful young nursing student when I first met her. She had been enrolled in the Eleanor Wade Custer School of Nursing at Shenandoah University where she attended classes at the Leesburg campus in northern Virginia and would ultimately graduate with her nursing degree in December 2015. She was the youngest of three siblings with two older compassionate sisters, Becky and Cathy, and two wonderful supportive parents, Wanda and Bill. What struck me the most was her determination, in spite of the cancer, to continue her dream of being a nurse. Not only was she carrying out a weekly routine which included driving back and forth between her parents' home in southern Virginia to attend classes two hours away in northern Virginia, but was getting cancer treatments in between, which sometimes landed her in the emergency room. She was determined to beat this illness so she could help other cancer patients like herself – something I greatly admired about her. She was one of the most gentle, caring, and empathetic individuals I have ever met and as you will see our relationship has continued long after her transition to the afterlife.

There was something special about Allison. She had a special light in her eyes and I could sense and feel an angelic energy about and within her. I knew she had been placed on this earth to help and teach others. She came to that first session open yet somewhat guarded and apprehensive about sharing her intimate details. I could tell she was afraid to say how she really felt about what was happening to her and how it was affecting others around her. She was unsure, like many who are dealing with similar conditions, about how to deal with the disease and the difficult choices it presented in terms of medical treatments. Recognizing this I opened the door ever so slightly and gave her the space without judgment to allow the fear, anger, and the confusion about what was happening to her to surface. Through our work together, I gently led her into exploring new ways of looking at what the cancer meant in terms of finding meaning, purpose, messages, and possibly 'gifts' for her and her family. This would empower her to 'own the disease' on both a physical and spiritual level and so our journey together began . . .

I knew one of the most important things I had to do from the start was get her reconnected to her body. This is a common thread for those who suffer from medical conditions and life-threatening illnesses as it is very hard to connect to a body you feel has betrayed you. There is a natural tendency for the human mind to detach from the part of the body where the disease is but what I have found is that our bodies hold the stories, and the insight, into what we need to do to take care of ourselves. It was my intent to help her get into her physical body and connect to what the pain had been holding for her.

As we began this process, she began to realize some of her pain held the stories linked to her life themes – themes she needed to complete before her transition from this lifetime. Emerging from this work were the themes of learning to speak her truth, stating her wants and needs openly and clearly, and releasing the fear of feeling like a burden to others. Allison worked through these themes and even proudly began to confront certain doctors who she felt treated her like a number rather than a living, breathing human being. At one point, we even discussed how she could integrate her experience as a nursing student and cancer patient within a curriculum I had designed and taught at Georgetown University for medical professionals. The curriculum focused on how stress, trauma, and life-changing events effect the physical, mental, emotional, energetic and spiritual components of an individual as well as how the importance of getting in touch with oneself as a provider can lead to improved patient care. Although this idea provided some comfort on an emotional level, there was also the immediate issue of alleviating the pain from the tumors.

In order to manage the pain, I taught her a foundational breathing technique based on the principles of Kundalini yoga that would help to calm the nervous system and reduce anxiety. I also taught her a 'grounding' technique, akin to visualization, whereby I have my clients anchor themselves to something higher or more powerful than themselves (i.e. nature) by conceptualizing parts of the body, usually the feet, as being rooted to the earth like trees. This process helps calm anxiety, reduces the fight-flight-freeze response, and ultimately brings clarity – an essential component, especially for those battling life-threatening illness, to help make well-informed choices for one's highest good.

Not only did Allison have to deal with excruciatingly painful tumors, so much so that by the last few weeks of her life she couldn't even tolerate the slightest movement of the bedsheets, but also difficult treatments, painful blood draws, insertion of ports, and several blood transfusions. She had concern about an upcoming blood transfusion as she had gotten very sick from the last one she received just prior to meeting me so we worked on how to prepare for the next one. I shared with Allison that when a person receives blood from someone else, they not only receive the actual blood but they also receive an imprint of the donor's energetic and vibrational level. I had Allison recognize this and taught her how to visualize clean, clear blood coming in this time with an energy level compatible with hers. This was the power of the mind to mitigate side effects, which worked as Allison reported feeling much better this time around.

Like many of my clients with medical conditions and life-threatening illnesses, Allison's condition required much more than simply alleviating pain. As much as I knew she would make a wonderful, loving, caring, and empathetic nurse, I also knew graduating from nursing school would be the last thing Allison would be able to accomplish from a physical standpoint in this lifetime. One of the hardest parts of this journey with her was to help her get in touch with and find meaning in the disease. As Allison and I got to know each other, I gave her the space she needed to explore this topic and challenged her to find meaning in the cancer. Why had it shown up? What was the purpose? What was it trying to teach her? My work has always been about finding the 'gifts' in trauma, as difficult and strange as that might seem. I try to help my clients find the deeper meaning behind the suffering and in Allison's case this meant going directly into the tumors in the body to find the meaning they held.

Working from the premise that stress, trauma, and life-changing events become lodged in the body, I took Allison to her heart center as I knew that was where the fear was lodged. As I gently guided her to bring her awareness to this area, she became aware that the fear her heart center was holding was about the pain this disease was giving her. She then moved into the pain to receive the message: *"I'm afraid of the pain but it wants me to trust it. How do I trust it?"* I then had her go into the place where her fear was stronger than her pain. Her body revealed to her that she was more than strong enough to handle it, which was the validation she needed to maneuver through this disease. All the while she was connecting to her physical body, her pain level dropped allowing her to breathe more calmly. She began to realize she felt worse when she ignored her body and the messages it was giving to her but when she did allow herself to hear what the messages were saying, her pain level subsided and she was able to gain clarity about her tumors, her pain, and her truth.

As Allison began to reconnect to her body through this technique, she would be the one to take the lead to identify which places in her body to explore and find the deeper meaning and messages of what they were holding for her. For instance, I remember when she was very nauseous and was having difficulty breathing. I had her bring her awareness to the tumor in her belly and had her focus on what it was telling her. The tumor in her belly told her that she didn't need to worry so much of what others thought and to be confident to voice her opinion. After the information came out, her nausea decreased, her breathing became easier, and she began speaking her truth to her family, friends and boyfriend. Through this process Allison was able to hear many messages the body had been holding for her long before the cancer had been diagnosed. She realized, like most people, that she had been pushing her body beyond its limits without listening to what the body could do or handle.

I witnessed a profound transformation in the way Allison not only conceptualized her illness but found the strength to endure as a result of our work together. When I first met her the question that was first and foremost on her mind was "why me?" After getting connected to her body and finding meaning in the disease, she went to a place of "why did I get chosen for this?" This began to open the door to discussing death and what might happen if she were to transition, which led to the final obstacle – facing death itself.

Having confronted the most challenging aspect of this disease, we then moved into the final obstacle and the curiosity she had about death. Although I had many experiences and stories I wanted to share with her about death, I knew she needed a segue to open the door for this kind of dialogue so I gave her the book 'Many Lives Many Masters' by Dr. Brian Weiss. I had studied under him years ago at the Omega Institute for Holistic Studies in upstate New York and found his insight into death and the afterlife congruous with my intuitive and clairvoyant gifts. Reading this book gave her a comfort level in talking about death and the afterlife, which then gave me the opportunity to share my stories of the messages I had received from those who had transitioned. Giving her the hope and knowing that there is something beyond this earthly existence and letting her know the soul never dies turned out to be the most powerful work we did together. This served as a turning point for Allison as she was beginning to dip her toe in the possibility of her own death.

From my experience, when an individual is going through severe medical conditions and everything in their life from their viewpoint has been taken away (can't eat, exercise, in too much pain, depression, can't be around people) the themes always arise – what is the suffering for, what is it all about, I don't believe in a God. What I have seen most of the time is that they haven't confronted, faced, or embraced their life themes and the messages their body has been giving them through the years. Instead as usual they have their brains tell the body to continue pushing on. The brain tells the body what it's going to do, how it's going to do it, and the length of duration, while at the same time keeping the emotions at bay. All of this lodges in every corner and crevice of the physical body.

On top of that, many have brought into this lifetime past traumas they weren't able to complete or deal with in previous lifetimes. This compilation from previous lifetimes into one's current lifetime explains why things will come to a head for the person experiencing a severe medical issue. They are learning it's a compilation of past medical, physical, and emotional trauma. I teach my clients it's okay to feel, connect, and embrace it. I also teach them there are bigger themes being integrated into this picture. As a patient dealing with a medical condition, it's not only about what they are learning but it's also about how they take what they are learning and pay it forward to whoever needs this information for their personal growth, whether it be their children, significant others, friends, etc. They are finding and passing on the gift and the messages in the condition.

As you will read throughout this book, I was born with the gift of being able to tap into the other side and have been able to use messages from beyond to inform the work I do here in the present. Allison transitioned from this world on Monday, February 15, 2016 and although she was not able to realize her dream of being a nurse in this lifetime, she is able to pursue this work from the other side in her spirit form. Since her transition, she has come to me several times and has given me specific images and messages for her family. It is a tricky balance for me to share the messages I get from beyond with people that are here but I sensed from the relationship I had with her mother Wanda that she would be open to it so I opened the door and began sharing Allison's messages with her. To give you an example, one time Allison described to me an image of where she would be sitting during the holidays at the family table and wanted me to pass this message along to her family so they would know she would be with them in spirit. I described the chair and its position to Wanda and was told this was the exact same chair and position Wanda had purposefully left empty as a reminder that her daughter was there.

I continue to receive messages like these for her family but she has also begun working in unison with me to assist my clients. When Allison enters my body I can feel her spirit moving right through me as she moves through my upper back to my heart center. The themes she shares with me encompass straddling this planet with other realms, what expansion of soul feels like, and how one can be in several places at one time. She now assists me with the work I do. While working with a client in March 2017 who was awaiting brain surgery, Allison came to me to offer assistance. As I stood with my hands on my client as she lay on the table I use for my healing sessions, I felt Allison's divine presence step inside my physical body. My body instantly felt lighter and healthier but my feet became heavier than usual. Allison was making sure I was grounded to the earth in the same way I help my clients ground themselves through their feet. I then felt Allison's divine presence enter my client's body and assist me with additional healing and support. This was a powerful example of how souls never die. They can come back and assist us here in this lifetime in many ways and forms but you have to be open to receiving it. All that Allison has brought to me and continues to bring, gets packed inside my Red Bag as I utilize these gifts to help others in a world where there is so much pain, illness, trauma and uncertainty.

I share this information with you as a beacon of hope that our loved ones, although maybe not here in physical form, are still here in a spiritual sense to help us, guide us, and provide meaning for our lives. I believe Allison's death, although heartbreaking, tragic, and much too early, was a means of helping all of us, learn valuable lessons about death and the afterlife. While writing this book, I received many messages from Allison but none more personal than the one I am about to share. She wanted her mother to know how much she appreciated her never leaving her side while she transitioned and the support she gave her throughout the entire process. She also wanted her mother to know how her death has brought Wanda and myself together for a joint purpose – and that is for those of you suffering from the grieving process to find hope and meaning through the dying process. So you see, the soul never dies. From beyond this earthly realm, Allison's wings continue to inspire.

6

AFTER THE TRANSITION:
A MOTHER'S MESSAGE

Over the course of my journey with Allison, I would come to know members of her family, especially her mother Wanda, with whom I forged a special and intimate relationship. As Allison and I would conduct our sessions over Skype, often times Wanda would pop in or drop by to say hello. When Allison's condition began to worsen after her graduation from nursing school, Wanda began to reach out to me personally on the side. What began as a few conversations here and there quickly turned into daily correspondence on how she could best support her daughter. As I had challenged Allison to find deeper meaning in the disease, I, too, challenged Wanda to consider expanding her belief system to include being open to the possibility of finding support in spiritual realms. I coached Wanda on how she could assist Allison in moving from this lifetime to the next and shared messages I received from the spirit world who provided guidance on the transition. I would like to think these conversations not only helped Wanda deal with the transition of her daughter but also gave her the space and opportunity to look at death differently. And more importantly I wanted her to trust her knowing that she did everything she could throughout Allison's illness and transition because it all came from a place of love.

As many of us have been touched by the passing of a loved one, and in some cases the painful experience of having lost a child, I reached out to Wanda to see if she would be open to share her experience. As a tribute to Allison and a way to make sure she continues to teach us even though she has left this physical world, I would like to include these words from Wanda to offer hope and provide a measure of comfort for those going through a similar experience. Let her words guide you through the grieving process and serve as a beacon of light that you may find peace and meaning within the suffering. I give you a mother's message . . .

Life is short and fragile . . .
God takes the loveliest flowers to be his own . . .
Some good will come from this . . .
Time will make things better . . .

Please remind me to never say these words to parents who have experienced the loss of a child. It is horrific . . . no matter what the age. I am in a quiet place, seven months since my beautiful daughter died from triple negative breast cancer that had metastasized throughout her body. I've been trying to understand all that has happened to our family. People pass by me, lost in their own little worlds . . . rushing about to soccer practice, to pick up groceries, to exercise at the gym, to get their car repaired . . . to go to church. They don't see my loss; they don't feel my pain . . . they aren't even aware of it. I wonder many times how lost my Allison felt as she faced each day of her diagnosis. We surrounded her with love, but in those dark recesses of time at the hour of the day when no one is with you . . . when your mind refuses to allow you rest . . . your brain just races with worst case scenarios . . . possibilities you cannot fathom. Young people are particularly resilient . . . even twenty-six year olds with dreams of a future life. As a nursing student, Allison knew the probabilities of her diagnosis, as well as the possibilities of remission. She also knew that she had to work as diligently as possible to complete her nursing degree; to keep working at her job as a dermatology assistant as often as she could. This kept her motivated to manage her treatments, and to keep thinking about the big picture . . . her future. Her completion of her nursing degree was nothing short of remarkable. The effort it required was astounding. I think she came to view her fight with cancer the same way . . . just keep working as hard as you can, and you will experience success.

Far too late in her diagnosis and treatment, she was convinced by a friend to seek the help of a therapist. We encouraged Allison over and over again to seek the counsel of a therapist, but it was only after a friend gave her a contact number that she sought out Paige Valdiserri, her emotional support and connection to her inner feelings. Paige opened doors for Allison; encouraged her to take control of her own emotional and personal life. Allison trusted Paige implicitly; I only wish she had been able to communicate longer with Paige. During her therapy with Paige, Allison repeated a passage that Paige had given her to read every morning while she faced herself in the mirror.

"I have all the time I need to do all I came to do and be in this lifetime. Just for today, I will trust that."

Allison repeated these words each morning. This helped her focus and hope for each day.

Allison was hospitalized for nearly six weeks at the end of her life. During the last approximately three weeks of

Allison's life, she was a patient in the Palliative Care Unit of Virginia Commonwealth University Hospital. This unit was designed to help both patients and families cope with the final days of their loved ones. It was in this unit that we were nurtured by a wonderful chaplain and attended to by many nurses and palliative care doctors. Their combined attention, care, and collective support helped us to navigate the sometimes exasperating procedures and treatments necessary. They also nurtured our spirits . . . our hearts; they gave us encouragement, hope, and a shoulder to cry on. According to Allison's oncologists and nurses, cancer in young people tends to progress quickly near the end of life. They suggested (two weeks prior to her death) that we call her oldest sister to come home to be with the family so that all of us could be together. It was a wonderful weekend, filled with celebration and laughter . . . and especially love. Her sister returned the following week to stay. We ate, slept, and cried together while sleeping in chairs or on a second room bed for those two weeks. We were all there (Mom, Dad and two sisters), but I kept feeling that my helplessness extended far beyond being able to help Allison's pain and her "knowing," even though she still refused to speak about death. It was then I started phoning Paige on a regular basis . . . many times during the day, in fact. I wanted to know how to help my daughter; how to make these days easier for her to face. After twelve months of chemotherapy treatment and radiation, Allison's cancer returned aggressively. Because her cancer manifested itself by forming muscular and dermal tumors throughout her body, she was in constant pain . . . an unnatural phenomenon in breast cancer patients. The oncologists were constantly reassessing procedure. The blood vessel system and the lymphatic system spread the cancer cells; but in Allison's case, the cancer cells kept mutating . . . ever changing, adapting to the chemotherapy and mutating into structurally different kinds of cells that could not be treated. Her pain escalated, but was partially controlled by IV pain meds. One night, during the last two weeks of her life, just the two of us were alone. She talked about her fears . . . "Do you think I am going to die? Should I make a list of things I want to go to my family and friends? Should I write letters . . . should I be afraid of dying?" These were all such difficult questions, and I did my best to answer them honestly, but I felt a need to allow her to feel hope. She did make statements to me instructing me how to distribute her personal things, clothes, and what little money she had. After a long discussion, she paused for a few moments and then said "I am going to keep fighting this . . . I am going to keep trying to beat this . . . " I reinforced this attitude, and told her that we would all support her decision whole heartedly. This was my personal decision . . . to continue to leave her hope intact.

The cancer had spread to her lungs, skull, and mandible . . . one day, at the beginning of her last week, she just couldn't drink or swallow. I think she knew how very serious her condition was, especially when a catheter was necessary. Still she refused to give up; she kept that beautiful smile on her face until she eased into a semi-conscious state. Paige counseled me via phone and urged us as a family to help Allison prepare to leave this physical world. Because Paige is clairvoyant, she was able to feel the presence of an angel in Allison's room . . . her dear friend, Jake, who had passed from this life ten years earlier. Many times during the past ten years, Allison had felt Jake's presence with her. She could not explain the "hows" or "whys" of her feelings, but she knew they were real. She always felt a special connection to Jake's spirit; he was always close to her. Little did we know that he would play such an important role in her own transition.

Taking a look back . . . I sometimes feel that I am in a dream state . . . usually when I first wake up. Then I remember . . . this is real; it did really happen. Cancer doesn't just happen to the patient . . . it happened to all of us in the family. My husband and I agonized over every detail of our daughter's treatment; her older sister, a physician, wanted to know every detail, every bloodwork report, and every doctor's consultation . . . every side effect experienced. She was so far away and felt so guilty for not being with Allison for every treatment. Our middle daughter tried to be here for every treatment; she was the "happiness" on a daily basis that we were all seeking . . . the person who tried to bring normalcy and laughter into everyone's life. Both daughters suffered great stress with their responsibilities. After the internet research and the second opinions; the treatments and surgeries . . . the cancer came back with determined acceleration. The worst was on its way, and we knew it . . . but could not fathom what that meant.

Watching someone you love as they die is an experience of some other dimension. You cannot stop what is happening. You must keep yourself from losing all grasp on reality while supporting the nuclear family and your loved one who is dying. In our situation, it was our beautiful, intelligent, compassionate daughter . . . just twenty-eight years old. All through her life, we held her hand before crossing the street; we kept every scheduled doctor's appointment; we taught her not to play with matches . . . not to accept rides with strangers . . . choose her friends carefully. We helped her pick up the pieces after an auto accident. We supported her through college and in her pursuit to become a nurse. But here we were . . . watching her slip away from us, and we were unable to do anything, or so we thought. The counsel given us by Paige was the most valuable, because it gave us direction so that we could help our daughter leave this physical realm of being and step in to the next. Since her soul will never die, she is somewhere. I believe she is helping others transition from this physical world into the next realm. She always was a caregiver; I believe she takes that with her . . . always helping others. As humans, we have no idea what possibilities await us. I choose to believe that there are unknown possibilities of happiness, everlasting life, and service that await us as our souls leave this earth.

Paige was instrumental in helping us during those last days. She advised us to keep talking to Allison . . . whispering into her ear continually as she slipped farther and farther away. So in the last four unconscious days, we stood by her side, caressing her, stroking her hands, feet . . . being as close to her as we possibly could. We kept whispering to her . . . these were personal, loving conversations, songs, moments of communicated love. We encouraged her to "step into the other realm," even just for a moment to experience what it would be like to feel the "light" of transitioning . . . to feel safe about allowing oneself to leave this earth. Paige advised us that Allison was still clinging to life and was afraid. Allison needed to "test" the waters a bit . . . allow herself to feel safe about leaving us. Whatever fears she may have had, we encouraged her to leave those fears behind . . . that her dear friend, Jake, who had died ten years earlier, was there with her in her room, ready to help her transition. Paige felt the presence of three other souls in Allison's room, but she could not identify them. I have since come to feel who they might have been, but these are my own comforting thoughts. Allison was young, and young people cling to life desperately. It was our role, as family members who loved her, to change the atmosphere of the room where our unconscious child lay breathing heavily. We knew her physical body was shutting down; it was her mind and soul we were trying to reach. I remember feeling less helpless and more empowered as a mother as I whispered to her. Sometimes, I sang a nursery rhyme or a familiar song that I sang to her as a child. Other times I reminded her that our love for her would continue every moment of every hour; every hour of every day, for the rest of our lives . . . even throughout eternity. We were there in constant state of awareness, yet not really understanding when her breath would become air. We were sending her on her way with as much love as we could put into words. I believe, as Paige does, that she could hear us . . . that she knew we were there . . . that she soaked up those whispered love offerings as the much needed confidence to take with her as she left us. The most important thing that we all gave her was "permission to leave us . . . "

When we realized that Allison was gone, that her soul had transitioned . . . we remained in her room, quietly talking about our beautiful girl. We held her for the last time, because we had been unable to touch her or caress her for fear of hurting her. Her tumors had been so painful that we could no longer embrace her. Even a wrinkle in her sheet could cause discomfort. It was so difficult to not touch her when all we wanted to do was hold her to make her feel better. We were numb, but we felt a certain kind of peace that it was finally over for her. Our own grief was just beginning. We didn't realize, that we had given her a most important gift. Paige had to point that out to us later. We had yet to realize that we had played a far-reaching role in her transition.

All through her last seventeen months on this earth, Allison tried to protect us . . . worried about us . . . didn't want us to give up our lives for her. She never wanted us to be sad or tearful. She hated the fact that she had caused such a disruption in our lives. She appreciated every act of love that we showed her . . . our presence at her treatments, our support during her surgical recoveries, our sacrifices (or what she considered to be sacrifices).We considered it our privilege to help take care of our child. I think that her determination to survive was her way of helping us face each day. She had a few friends that had not contacted her or supported her, but she never held it against them. She was the most compassionate and forgiving person that I have ever known. As I look back on all that she endured, I am overwhelmed with her constant positive attitude . . . her desire to look to the future . . . her need to believe in hope and to show us that she believed in it. Why is it that such a beautiful person should be taken from us? This is a question that I cannot answer, nor do I think anyone can. I am very wary of people who have all of the answers; I do not believe that we can know, at least not yet. Perhaps, when we transition ourselves, things will be made clearer.

Throughout these past eight months since my daughter's passing, I have traveled, sometimes uncontrollably, the gamut of grieving, and the process is still going on. In the beginning, there was a physical pain in my heart which I could feel . . . an aching, longing, actual pain that pervaded every moment. This feeling is still present sometimes, although less frequently. In the beginning, I was angry, unhappy, sad, overcome, overwhelmed . . . afraid to go out in public for fear it was disrespectful to my daughter. I was afraid to laugh out loud; afraid to feel any joy for fear it would be viewed as unnatural or not the proper thing to express. It was a confusing, frustrating, horribly sad time in my life. I just lost all control at times. The last tortured days of her life were constantly showing up in my mind's eye. I could concentrate on nothing save the cruelty of her disease and how cancer took her away from me . . . from all of us. My mind would just be focused on thinking of her, remembering how she looked; thinking of her suffering and the procedures she had to endure. No beautiful, compassionate, loving child should ever have to experience that kind of pain and physical deterioration. The "whys" of this experience still overwhelm me. Constantly, I am reminded of several important factors . . . my husband needs me, my two adult children need me, my grandson needs me . . . They all need me in different ways; they especially need the solid strength of their Dad and his pragmatic way of looking at life as a gift. Each of our family members is coping with this loss in a very personal way. Each one of us must face each day and hold these events in our hearts forever. I have come to the realization that my most important goal now is to take care of myself, physically, so that I can help my living children feel less afraid about life, less fearful of death, and help them to accept their sister's life in the next realm, and her peaceful existence. What we need to strive to do is to figure out how to live in this life, finding our own peace and place in this world. Each one of us, in our family, must travel this journey of grief and healing at our own pace and in our own manner. There is no time table; there is no method that will shorten the terrible, no good, very bad times.

"They say" that keeping busy is important. Whoever "they" are have a decent point. I do try to keep busy; I need to keep my mind occupied with ideas that matter. My husband is still working; his busy optometric practice is enjoyable to him. He loves his encounters with people and helping them. I have several really wonderful friends who have worked diligently to keep me engaged. The birth of our first grandchild has become a joy with untold benefits; fears and sadness melt away when we see or hold him. I feel my daughter, Allison's, presence many times when I am with him. I once read an anonymous quote "Whatever be your longing or your need . . . that give; then shall your soul be fed and you indeed will live." I have always remembered that quote, and I believe that it is true. What we need in this life, we must give to others . . . whether it be love, compassion, forgiveness, or our presence . . . a listening ear, a shared sorrow, or a loaf of bread. Whatever we extend to others is what helps us to find our own peace and self-worth.

As I read "Many Lives, Many Masters" by Brian L. Weiss, M.D., I am comforted through much of what was written about a young woman whose past lives were revealed in therapy sessions with the doctor. The memories she has of dying and being reborn give a great deal of information about what our spiritual world may require of us. The "masters" who speak through the young woman in therapy spoke of the lessons we must learn in this physical life. According to these spirits, "Everybody's path is basically the same. We all must learn certain attitudes while we're in the physical state. Charity, hope, faith, love . . . we must all know these things and know them well." If it is true, that by knowledge, we approach God, then I shall keep trying to learn. I do believe that Allison's spirit . . . her soul . . . transitioned to a place of peace with her family and friends waiting for her. These dear souls helped her to transition; they are with her now. I believe that she is traveling a great expanse that I cannot even envision . . . that she no longer feels pain or disappointment. She learned so many lessons in her short lifetime; she was our teacher, also. I know that I have much to learn and experience, but my grief will interrupt me sometimes. Just when I think I have a handle on maintaining some sort of normalcy, I dissolve again. The hurt is always with you; you must choose to power through, because we are just trying to get through this one day . . . loving, forgiving, helping, caring, understanding, and reaching for new experiences in finding our patience and peace. I believe that Allison found that peace.

The thoughts and the words written in this chapter are mine entirely. I cannot write about my husband's grief or that of my two living daughters. They must think about and work through their own grief, an extremely personal journey. I cannot visit their innermost thoughts, although we do talk about Allison and how we are coping. I know that they are suffering, and I try to do the best that I can to help them. Even though I would like to remove this terrible grief from them, I cannot do this. They each have their own memories of the final days of our beautiful Allison. Her suffering haunts us all, but we grieve differently. I will say that we are improving; we have decided to keep on living and breathing . . . planning and working. We have made a promise to ourselves to live our lives in a way that would honor our daughter and sister. We must do this every day, or we could not live with ourselves. Writing these thoughts as I have done is my way of honoring Allison; it is my way of coping with this terrible loss. There is still so much to understand and so much love to give others. I have made a promise to our Allison that I will continue to love her every moment of every hour; every hour of every day for as long as I live. Then I will love her throughout eternity. Because it is in loving her so completely that she lives with me every day. And that is so important to me.

Seven more months have passed by; it is now fourteen months since our Allison transitioned. Our grief, as a family, has gone through a kind of transition . . . change is thrust upon you. You must go on working, speaking, being a part of a whole, interacting with others . . . you don't have a choice. Men and women grieve differently; siblings have their own path to travel but their grief is no less intense or heartfelt than a mother's or a father's. How grief manifests itself in your body, heart, and mind is so personal. You cannot "tame" it; it has a life of its own. The important thing to say here and now is that we are looking forward to the future as if it has meaning and purpose. We are trying our best to live the kind of life that would honor our daughter, Allison. We are all looking to find that particular kind of help that we each need. My husband and I have stayed married. Paige tells me that the death of a child can tear a couple apart. We are blessed that we used our love to help one another. We strive to help our adult children, but they each are traveling a journey of grief that is their own. We can talk about Allison now, remembering special events and fun times we shared together. Each of her siblings treasures the wonderful experiences they had with their sister; it is really second nature to them to daily remember. I have given my daughters a card which has a verse that I have suggested that they read each day:

"Just for today, I will trust in my knowledge . . .
that your soul lives and works for good. I will trust
that you watch over me . . . I will honor you by living
with integrity, courage, compassion and love . . . just as
you did. I will be happy as I know you want me to
be.I will remember you with love and gratitude and
let my sadness ease."

61

Allison is still an extension of our very souls.

Paige has been instrumental in my progress; my connection with her is intensely personal. Her calm demeanor and deep understanding of grief and transition have helped me to come to terms with my own feelings and expectations. She has helped me to understand how Allison is joyous in her new realm. I feel very strongly that Allison is working through Paige to help her with this book and her clients. I also feel that Allison wanted me to write what I have written so that it might help others. Innocent, decent people suffer tragedies all of the time. These tragedies or illnesses, even deaths, are not caused by God. Sometimes bad things happen to people for no reason; there is randomness in the world. We were not bad people; we were not being punished for some previous ill act . . . we were just parents and siblings who lost their daughter and sister to a cruel disease. As hurt as we are, everyone faces hurt, disappointment, loss and tragedy in their lives. Perhaps it is not that we must know why these terrible things happen, but, rather, have some clearer understanding of how we must respond to them. Paige has suggested that I must see the "larger picture here . . . that there is so much more going on than we can possibly know." So I am constantly trying to look beyond the moment and our own personal tragedy . . . seeing the goodness and Christ like qualities of our friends, the people who treated Allison and cared for her, trying to save her life. I am hoping that through my determination to ask the important questions in life, I am honoring her memory. We are here to help one another; it's as simple as that. Through my pain, perhaps I can better ask you "How can I help you?" It's what Allison would want; it was her compassion that brought her to the decision to become a nurse. Most of us have only begun to tap our abilities to be charitable, to love, to have hope and faith, and to live unselfishly . . . doing without expectation of receiving anything in return. Allison taught me so much during her life in this physical world, and she continues to teach me. I am learning something new every day . . . trying to see beyond my own grief, bringing purpose and understanding into my life. This is a journey . . . my duty to honor Allison.

Wanda Ryan,
mother of Allison Virginia Ryan

7

LIFE INTERRUPTED

D o you want to be here anymore?" I asked my husband, all the while knowing the answer.

It was the hardest question I'd ever had to ask anyone, especially someone I loved so deeply. The possibility of death had now come to our doorstep for the third time. As our eyes welled with tears, his answer rang through me to the core. He was done. He was completely worn out and hopeless after the many years of doing everything he could do to get better and didn't want to keep living this way in constant illness. That question, however, opened the door for him to speak about what he had been feeling deep down inside but was too afraid to share. His pride and his ego kept stuffing the emotions down and prevented him from sharing this true vulnerability with me.

I told him I wanted him to stay but whatever he needed to choose I would support. I knew straddling the two worlds of having one foot in life and the other in death wouldn't work for him anymore. He was at a crossroads. If he wanted to be here in this lifetime then he had to be here fully no matter what that looked like. If, on the other hand, he was ready to go, then he had to begin embracing that piece of his journey. Either way, I was there for him. As I look back on this time in our lives, it occurs to me my life was mirroring the way I came into this world. I was once again straddling the worlds of life, sickness, death, and psychic realms. My life had come full circle.

November 2010

Two months before my husband began what would be almost a four-year battle with a mystery illness, I was lying in bed next to him in our home in Alexandria, Virginia when I was abruptly shown a vision of him in a coffin with me looking down at him. Throughout my life I have often been shown visions right before they would happen, so you can imagine the uneasiness I felt with this image. It was challenging lying next to him, not being able to share the image and emotions I was experiencing, but I did. Since it was particularly disturbing, I shared it with a friend of mine who was familiar with my mystical gifts. Her response was again validation for me of how fearful people are around the topic or possibility of death. She had minimized it and told me it was nothing, yet, deep down I knew something was coming.

That January (2011), my husband and I traveled to Maya Tulum, Mexico with my good friend and her husband along with several folks from her yoga studio for a yoga retreat. I had been in the middle of my Kundalini yoga certification program at the time so this trip was perfect timing. Prior to the trip, my husband and I had many deep discussions about where we were in our marriage, how I had put some of my long-term goals and dreams on the back burner so to speak to support him not only financially but emotionally through his many ventures. The first part of our marriage had revolved more around his needs than mine or ours together. 2011 would finally be the time where I could step out and be supported on the next part of my journey, which included continuing to work towards adoption, since I wasn't able to conceive. We both agreed this time was long overdue.

During the retreat, we attended a Native American sweat lodge ceremony one evening with our friends. The ceremony was held on the beach inside a large, tepee-like structure by a wonderfully spiritual and gentle Native American man. As we entered the tepee and the cloth door closed, we sat side-by-side in a very intimate circle surrounding a ceremonial fire pit. Amongst the darkness you could see the smoldering ashes in the fire pit, the outlines of those in the circle and the shadows of who was sitting right next to you. When the ceremony began, we were asked to put an intention out to the universe as to what we wanted to shift, change, or manifest in our lives and were encouraged to say it out loud as we went around the circle. As I waited my turn to speak, I was thinking about all I wanted to do in the world to make a positive difference.

While the list kept growing in my head of all the things I wanted to manifest and the excitement began to mount, my husband began to speak. As his words came out, my jaw hit the floor, my heart began to pound, and everything I was going to voice left me instantly. This man, my husband, stated he wanted to be a better man and a better husband to and for his wife. He proclaimed in front of the group I had sacrificed a lot for him and our marriage and this was something I deserved. I was in complete shock and taken off guard. To hear these words which he had never expressed before and was now professing to a group of mainly strangers save for two of our friends, cut through the whole fiber of my being as I melted in the sheer love and authenticity of his words. He had voiced them so clearly and articulately and with such conviction that the universe could not be mistaken about what he wanted for me and for us. This was the first time in our marriage where I knew undeniably he wanted to be there for me. But as moving and powerful as the occasion was for me, the words and intentions Tim shared that night in the dark tepee would put into motion the most challenging four years of our lives.

A couple of weeks after we returned from our trip, Tim began experiencing disturbing physical symptoms. He began waking up early in the morning before his alarm and would be unable to get back to sleep. He began experiencing nervousness and anxiety in the mornings and found it difficult to concentrate at work. Simple tasks he had taken for granted such as responding to emails, comprehending what he was reading, and even being able to put thoughts together and express them clearly were now challenging. In addition, he began losing weight rapidly, his appetite shrank, and he became easily fatigued. It got to the point where he had to cancel some baseball coaching clinics on the weekends because his body couldn't physically handle it. I remember him coming home in March of that year with a look of sheer panic as he told me he tried to throw batting practice and thirty pitches left him keeled over in exhaustion. (*He used to throw 200-300 pitches a night at practice several times a week.) We would go for walks around the block and he would come home and sink on the couch in sheer exhaustion. We were both extremely scared. Something was very wrong.

His symptoms kept getting progressively worse. He found it very difficult to concentrate at work and would call me multiple times throughout the day to help him deal with it. He would describe his symptoms as being on a giant roller coaster in that he would wake up in the morning with tremendous fear and anxiety but his symptoms would subside by mid-afternoon and he would feel "normal" again. But the fatigue got to the point where he had to stop coaching baseball and began cutting back at work. Up until this point I don't think he had ever taken a 'sick' day from work and that included teaching middle school and high school, which is not only one of the most exhausting professions but schools are havens for germs. His weight continued to plummet and his hands and feet would sweat profusely. These symptoms progressed to the point where he had great difficulty remembering people's names, something he was ordinarily good at, and could barely string a sentence together. I can't tell you how difficult it was to watch this happen. I remember very vividly one day in particular when the two of us were sitting at the kitchen table and I was trying to engage him in conversation. His mind just couldn't take in and comprehend what I was saying. It was at this point a profound sadness swept over me as I realized the partner I once had to share my thoughts, feelings, and simple mundane trivialities of the day could no longer be there for me in the way he once had. However, it was clear to me something physiologically was affecting his brain and I held out hope that with the right medical care he would be able to return to what he had been before.

These symptoms couldn't have come at a worse time for us as we had just begun the adoption process through Catholic Charities and were scheduled for a series of home visits. We had a home visit in late March with the social worker and we both feared his condition would exclude us from being admitted as potential adoptive parents. We had already been through several heartbreaks with the adoption process, including two girls from Iraq and a beautiful little baby boy in Rwanda whom I had met and held on a site visit during my People-to-People delegation, so we were obviously fearful. I placed Tim in a chair in our family room and told him to just sit there and nod. "Don't say a word," I said. "I'll do the talking."

Fortunately this was a very brief visit as we had already complied with the necessary paperwork and just needed to secure the home visit. After she left, I put Tim in the car and drove him up to the Emergency Room at Johns Hopkins University Hospital in Baltimore, Maryland. I called his parents who live in Delaware to meet us there, which they did. I had chosen this hospital for its excellent reputation but unfortunately our experience was not what we had hoped. After waiting several hours since my husband's case was not considered an "emergency," we were given a doctor who, despite the numerous physiological symptoms, suggested this might be a case of bipolar disorder. As a therapist, I knew damn well this wasn't a mental illness but rather something physiologically effecting his brain. Our trip to Johns Hopkins left us more frustrated than when we started. This was the first sign of the difficulties of finding a solution or course of treatment through the Western system of medicine – a theme that will emerge throughout this book. It was also the day that began a long, exhaustive four-year journey of medical research, full-time caregiving, daily emotional support and crisis management, support beyond this earthly realm, lessons in personal growth, ongoing depletion of money due to medical costs, and an exhaustive coordination of medical care through several integrative doctors to figure out this complex and multidimensional illness.

After the disappointing episode with the hospital, I immediately began researching doctors who utilize integrative medicine approaches. These doctors focus on the whole person, as well as aspects of lifestyle, and make use of a variety of therapeutic approaches by healthcare professionals and professions to achieve optimal health and healing. Integrative doctors emphasize the relationship between the practitioner and the patient, which is how I operate in my own practice so it was only natural I would gravitate in this direction. I found a practice in the Washington, D.C. area which I had utilized a few years before to treat my own symptoms from uranium exposure in Iraq. There were so many things going wrong in his body it was difficult to figure out where to begin. This would take years and multiple doctors, as well as many providers from across the wellness spectrum.

With such a complex illness and multiple areas of his body shutting down, each time one area was being treated, another would go by the wayside. One piece of the puzzle was the identification of a life-threatening complication regarding his thyroid. His ongoing persistent sweating, shaking, restlessness, confusion, and palpitating heart were indicative signs he was experiencing a 'thyroid storm.' This condition is a form of accelerated hyperthyroidism or thyrotoxic crisis which requires immediate emergency care. I can't tell you how many times during that first year he would spiral into a thyroid storm and would need my help to get him immediate care. As these doctors tried to balance his thyroid, other medical issues arose which would prevent it from stabilizing completely.

We were fortunate to have three doctors within the practice evaluate and provide analysis for his condition. Although each one was responsive, caring, and informative, what was needed for the best course of treatment was collaboration between the three and this didn't happen. Presumably one of the doctors held himself in higher regard, thus, despite my best efforts to get them to communicate with each other, he refused. This was the same doctor who charged $400USD per fifteen-minute phone session. You can imagine the stress I was under to have all the facts and questions prepared ahead of time to make sure we maximized each minute. Coordinating this medical care while working two jobs was beyond draining. Not only did I have to stay on top of the doctors but had to continually research additional medical treatments while providing caregiving and reporting ongoing updates to friends and family. As the medical bills piled up and his situation became more precarious, it felt like we were plugging up holes in a dam without finding the major leak. This would change when I was led to our next doctor.

I had always been divinely led to whom I needed to take Tim to next, which brought us to an incredible doctor, Dr. Hai Jin Kim in Annandale, Virginia in early September. By this time he was at his lowest weight, 127 lbs. on a 5'11 frame, and resembled a walking skeleton. When I would hug or hold him, all I would feel were bones. His memory and comprehension had also been worsening which meant I had to repeat things over and over on a daily basis as if I were talking to an Alzheimer's patient. In this condition, it was hard for him to feel valuable and at times I could feel the light within him slowly fading. Not being able to work and carry out the functions of everyday tasks began to wear on him as I could feel his sense of self-worth diminishing. Sensing this, I gave him simple tasks to do around the house so he could get a feeling of contributing but they required repeated instructions and were often met with great frustration. Even simple tasks like vacuuming, folding laundry, and doing chores around the house were challenging. It was as if my husband was now my child.

As we began working with Dr. Kim, she continued to work on stabilizing his thyroid but also came up with a huge piece of the puzzle as to the root cause of some of his other symptoms such as loss of appetite, hair loss, extreme fatigue, severe weight loss, anxiety and short term memory issues. She had us test our home for mold as she believed his symptoms were indicative of possible mold exposure. I immediately went to ACE Hardware and bought an inexpensive $10.00 mold testing kit and began the process. A few weeks after sending the test kit to the lab, we received confirmation that we had high levels of mold, especially three of the most dangerous kinds: Black Mold, Aspergillosis and Penicillium. These types of toxic mold can suppress and destroy the immune system, infiltrate the lungs, spread to the kidneys and cross over the blood-brain barrier into the brain causing all sorts of damaging, and potentially life-threatening, health issues. This would prove to be a pivotal piece of the puzzle in Tim's illness as we found out through genetic testing he lacks the genetic component necessary for detoxifying mold.

Given this new piece of information and the urgency of getting the mold removed, I quickly moved to hire a mold remediation company for our home. In order for the house to be remediated, we would have to move out for at least twenty-four hours which meant I had to find a hotel which accommodated pets and had to pack up our belongings, as Tim's anxiety and confusion rendered him unable to help. While coordinating the entire move I had to deal with a crisis at work as one of our employees in Iraq had experienced a traumatic situation and was in need of constant assistance. At this point, you could say this was synonymous with how my life had become – working with traumatic situations at work, helping clients with their traumatic issues in my own business, all the while living daily with my own personal traumatic situation.

After the mold remediation had been completed we moved back into a house that was free and clear of mold, or at least, that's what we were promised. Tim began to slowly show signs of improvement and went back to work on a part-time basis in October. Although we both thought this could be the beginning of a full recovery, unfortunately it wouldn't last. His symptoms began returning in December and returned in full force by January to the point where he was forced to take family medical leave. This time it would be for eight excruciating months.

When we returned to Dr. Kim, we were confused and scared as to why this was recurring. She had been treating him with a mold protocol which required an oral medication to bind the toxins and flush them out of his system. When his symptoms became worse, she suggested we have the mold company come back and re-test the house to verify all of the mold had been remediated. When the results came back in, you can only imagine the fire in my belly when they casually told us they hadn't removed all of the mold, particularly from a spot in our upstairs bathroom. So now I had to get him out of the environment and quickly.

Since mold is extremely difficult to fully remediate, Dr. Kim suggested the best option for his health would be for us to move permanently out of our home. At this point I had no choice but to pack our belongings, find a place to rent, and put our house on the market. While I continued to work two jobs, the stress and magnitude of the situation became unbearable. Even though we had help along the way from some friends and Tim's family, I needed assistance above and beyond this earthly realm to carry me through. I called out to the universe, my angels, my guides, the Divine, and my grandmother for help. One night shortly thereafter I remember waking up screaming from a dream as I felt myself laying in a coffin that I couldn't get out of while dirt was being thrown on me. It was evident this dream represented the feeling of being buried alive with more and more responsibilities being piled upon me. After the nightmare as I left our bedroom and stood in the bathroom, a strong message came in the form of a smell of the perfume Windsong by Prince Matchabelli, which my grandmother used to douse herself with when she was alive. The smell began as a light fragrance but soon began to engulf every piece of me as I felt her strong and loving presence. She was with me once again letting me know I wasn't alone and that I had support from the other side. She would continue to show up in this manner in the bathroom with her perfume as a daily reminder.

As I began to pack our home an intense sadness filled me. This was a home and community I had loved for the past nine years and I wasn't ready to leave but I knew if we didn't, my husband might die. A challenging range of emotions would trigger in me the sacrificing I had already done throughout our whole marriage and the selfishness I felt for having these feelings. This along with many other emotions would plague me throughout his illness as his wife and caregiver.

While driving to get boxes at the UPS store for packing, a second message showed up from beyond this earthly realm. This time it came in the form of an animal. Just as I packed the boxes in my car and put the top down, I saw two beautiful bald eagles flying above. They flew directly above me as if they were escorting me back to the house. Whenever I stopped for traffic signals or stop signs, they would circle above the car and wait for me to move again. This continued the entire way back to the house. I knew from my study of Shamanism and animal totems, the Eagle has always been one of my spirit animals that has traveled with me throughout my life reminding me of my purpose and my higher meaning. All creatures in nature have a specific type of energy, message, and meaning that show up in our path divinely to give us clarity, specific messages and understanding of our life's circumstances. We are not on this earth exclusive of nature; we are a part of it and live in unison with all forms of it. Birds symbolize the soul, the bridge between Earth and the Divine, and the elevation of consciousness. Eagle specifically teaches and reminds us of a heightened responsibility of spiritual growth and healing. They alert us that challenges are on the way and to summon the courage to prepare the inner strength and fortitude to meet them. With their ability to move between the earthly realm and the spirit world, they teach us to see things from a higher level. Once again I would pack these messages in my Red Bag not only to help on my current journey but to tuck away for my higher purpose of assisting others.

Life in the new apartment was an adjustment. Selling the house took more time and energy than I had to exert. Eventually we were able to sell our house, which was a huge blessing financially, but the move was extremely difficult with Tim's condition and it was extremely sad for me as I wasn't ready to leave my home. As we signed the paperwork with the new buyers, the process should have had a celebratory tone but for me all I could feel was sadness and grief. My life had been turned upside down. My husband's health was in a terrible state, we had to move out of the community where I felt at home, and my long-term goals of developing my healing business were in serious jeopardy, not to mention the fact that the adoption process and my hope of becoming a mother had to be put on hold once again. It was an extremely difficult time for me emotionally.

Although we were in a mold-free environment, Tim's medical condition was still precarious. He was following Dr. Kim's mold protocol and getting some of his energy back but still had extreme difficulty concentrating and comprehending. After several months with seemingly little progress and beginning to question if the mold treatment was the best course of action, especially since it was viewed with suspicion from a Western medicine standpoint, we finally resorted to hospitalization where he had a team of seven doctors, including a gastroenterologist, review his case. As I left the hospital that evening returning home with Tim's parents by my side, I laid in bed that night feeling the empty space without him. In my mind and in my heart, I felt as if I had to begin preparing for him not being in my life. I embraced the sad, lonely, empty, and dark feeling of what it would be like if he were to die. I spent most of the night trying to prepare for something that no one can truly prepare for, but I felt the need to begin the process, quietly and by myself.

The next day the doctors released him without being able to pinpoint the root cause. This news came with a double-edged sword as it might sound like good news that they weren't able to find anything but the bad news was there was no definitive diagnosis that we could identify and treat accordingly. Although this left us with a sense of more doubt, and at times hopelessness, it did reinforce the confidence we had in Dr. Kim and the mold diagnosis. We continued to work with her and kept following the mold protocol as she never gave up on trying to treat this multi-faceted illness with no 'one-size-fits-all' diagnosis.

Not having a definitive diagnosis from a Western medicine standpoint made it extremely challenging to deal with on many fronts. For one, we found it very difficult to explain the severity and complexity to friends, family, and colleagues. It also made it very difficult to predict or anticipate a timeline as to when Tim would get better and be able to return to work, which was the most frustrating aspect of this illness for him. This also hit us financially as he was denied short-term disability despite twenty-six pages of documents, medical tests, and letters from our doctors supporting the treatment. Above all, it was the uncertainty surrounding the nature and course of treatment that plagued us on so many levels. Without a definitive diagnosis to function as a 'guidebook,' we felt like we were swimming in unchartered waters once again.

As the summer crept up on us, so did the horrible storms and humid temperatures. The storms that summer seemed to be more violent than usual, with several causing major power outages – something we were accustomed to growing up on the east coast. However, there was one major storm in mid-July that wiped out power for several days leaving Tim's fragile body and compromised immune system in a precarious position. Amidst the sweltering heat of 100° temperatures and without air-conditioning, I once again felt desperate and helpless with the inability to do anything for him that is until I noticed about half of the rental units in our townhome complex appeared to have power. I pleaded with management to allow us to move in temporarily into one of the unoccupied units until power was restored, despite being against rental policy. Once again, divine assistance and human kindness prevailed as we were granted permission.

After the storms passed and we moved back into our original unit, Tim began settling into a routine which had him reading in the morning and going for nature walks in the afternoon and evenings. Although still under medical care his condition began to improve to the point where he was able to work part-time from home. That summer he organized a Labor Day 12U baseball tournament that brought together several D.C. area Little League teams from all parts of the District for the D.C. Department of Parks & Recreation and pulled it off successfully – a good win for the District and a personal victory for himself. Afterwards, he gradually worked his way back to full-time status at work.

Throughout this journey that began with the sweat lodge in Maya Tulum, the universe had been preparing us for something different. As things were being taken away from us – health, home, the security and stability of our old lives and the heartbreaking possibility of not becoming parents – we were being divinely led in a new direction. Tim and I had talked about making a fresh start in a place that could support his recovery but we weren't sure where this would be or what it would look like. During the summer of 2012, I traveled several times to Phoenix, Arizona for a professional certification course in Biodynamic Craniosacral Trauma Therapy where I befriended one of my classmates who grew up in Tucson. After hearing about Tim's condition and all we had been through the last two years, she suggested we look into moving out there. During one of my trips, she and I had a chance to spend the day in Tucson, where I received another clear message – this time from the mountains. The beautiful Catalina Mountains spoke to me with such clarity and force telling me to pack our belongings and bring Tim here to heal. As soon as I returned to the east coast, we found a realtor in Tucson and the process began.

As the thought of making a new start gave us some hope and optimism, we booked a trip to Tucson over the

Veteran's Day holiday weekend and spent three days exploring the area for a possible move. At the eleventh hour on our final day, we found a development in the northwestern suburb of Oro Valley with a beautiful view of the Catalina Mountains – the same mountains that spoke to me telling me to move Tim out here. As we drove into the development to meet with the sales representative, three baby bobcats ran across the road right in front of our car. That sealed the deal. We purchased the lot and had a spec home built.

The home we purchased had a completion date of April 2013 so you can imagine my surprise when I received a phone call in January saying it would be ready a month early in March. When do you ever hear of a house being completed a month ahead of schedule? It was another clear message that we needed to leave the east coast sooner than later. There was a bigger hand at work here. As such, we would need to fly out in February to sign the papers before the move in March.

On the day of the signing, it just so happened Tucson got 3-4 inches of snow. This usually occurs in the mountains but for this to happen in the valley was a fluke (or not). After we signed the papers, we headed back to our new home where we met the building superintendent, Frank, who had been great to work with throughout the whole process. As we got out of our rental car, Frank met us on the driveway with an extremely anxious look on his face. He asked if either of us had been in the house that morning. This seemed like a strange question since we hadn't received the keys to the house yet, as this was the entire point of us meeting him there. When we said no, I asked him if everything was okay. He then told us that when he had gone through the house for a final walk-through before our arrival, he came across something he couldn't explain. On the second floor balcony, which has only one access point from the master bedroom, he found a perfect angel formation embedded in the snow. As there were no footprints leading to or from, he couldn't understand how anyone could have made this without going through the house. As Frank was sharing this story with us, I smiled knowing intuitively it was a message from Archangel Michael who often travels with me and assists me with my clients. It was another clear sign we were right where we were supposed to be.

Even though the snow angel gave us a sense of peace and comfort about moving across country, it really hit me when we got back to Virginia just how much I was going to miss my clients and the business I had grown. Each night after my last client would leave, I would lay down on my office floor and cry as I wasn't ready emotionally to leave my work, my clients, and the office I loved so much. Although I wasn't ready to leave, I knew the universe was pushing us in the right direction with great force and I needed to trust and accept we were being led for the highest good of us both.

The move to Tucson in March was physically and emotionally taxing for both of us. Although Tim slowly eased back into work as a substitute teacher and taught a summer Biology course for the local school district while he looked for full-time work, his health had never fully recovered and he quickly went downhill after the summer course concluded in July. He still had yet to gain any weight and was once again experiencing difficult periods of nervousness, anxiety, great confusion, and fatigue. Since we did not have a doctor, Dr. Kim was kind enough to offer long-distance support as she knew we were in a new place without a support system. Although he had returned to work for several months and we both thought the coast was clear, this final leg of the illness would turn out to be the most challenging and the most difficult by far. Throughout this journey we had seen several health care providers, including integrative doctors who specialized in mold and autoimmune disease, but his illness reached a point by late July that both Dr. Kim and I felt the hospital was his last option.

As I stood next to Tim's hospital bed, I could feel the light and the hope slipping from his body. I began this chapter with a question I asked him in the Oro Valley hospital: "Do you want to be here in this lifetime anymore?" I braced for the answer I knew was coming. Although he didn't specifically say he wanted to die, he told me he didn't want to go on if he had to continually live like this. For someone as high-achieving and motivated as him, not being able to physically and mentally carry out the personal and professional work he was doing with youth and be as fully functioning as he had once been was beyond devastating. His spirit was crushed. I had been feeling it for years but in that hospital room, I felt it beyond reproach. Out of the many times we graced death's doorstep, I believed this could be our last and final time.

After bringing him home from the hospital I immediately called his parents and urged them to come out, as Tim's condition was dire. They had always seen me as a strong person who could handle just about anything but by this time the emotional fatigue and hopelessness was getting too much to bear. Although the illness and our subsequent course of treatment had been very challenging for them as the symptoms hadn't fit neatly into a Western diagnosis, they were more than willing to come out and support me by taking the burden of constant care off of my back which I greatly appreciated. Tim's mom ended up staying with us for the entire month. It was during this time that she could finally see and feel what it felt like for me to have to deal with the daily crises, the heavy challenges, and the fearful moments of what had been going on behind closed doors. The raw emotions of my caregiving were being laid bare for her.

There was one evening in particular in August where she and my husband finally got to see my vulnerability and feel the emotional burden this had been taking on me. Tim's brother Ryan had called one night to speak with my mother-in-law. During the course of the conversation, he told her how he thought all Tim needed to do was see a Western doctor and take certain medications. As she relayed this information, I could feel myself snap inside. In essence, he was questioning my entire approach as to how I was and had been taking care of my husband over the last three and a half years. In that moment, I completely lost it. I screamed at the top of my lungs how no one who hasn't walked this journey with me every step of the way would be able to offer quick-fix solutions. All the years of caregiving, researching medical options, and holding the space financially and emotionally, spewed out uncontrollably. I had never yelled or screamed like that in my entire life. Both Tim and his mom could not believe what they were seeing and hearing. I finally ran out of the house, down the driveway, and through the neighborhood until I couldn't run anymore. I remember looking up and seeing all the beautiful, crisp, clear stars in the Arizona sky and feeling a release of the pain, frustration, and anger which had culminated inside of me for these past years.

Eventually I walked my way back to the house to find my mother-in-law sitting outside saddened and worried while Tim had gotten in the car to search for me. I felt bad because he hadn't been in any condition to deal with the stress and fear I had just shown but they could finally feel and understand what I had been holding in. I sat with my mother-in-law on the couch and cried. For the first time she could see my vulnerability and my fragility. Although she had always been there for support, she said she now fully understood what I had been going through and what it must have been like to carry such a burden for so long. She also acknowledged how much I had done for her son and thanked me for taking such good care of him. By this time, Tim had returned. I ran to him, held him, and apologized for scaring him. He said he, too, hadn't realized how much was going on inside me and the extent of the heavy load I had been carrying. It was in that moment that my husband and mother-in-law would truly begin to understand a caregiver's journey.

Throughout my life I have been divinely-led and nowhere has this been more apparent than through this medical journey. After we had returned home from the Oro Valley hospital in late July and were left yet again with few answers, another message came to us in the form of two new neighbors. We had been walking through the neighborhood one afternoon when we stopped to talk to two neighbors who had just moved in. As I was describing Tim's illness, they told me their son had gone through something similar and they had found a fantastic naturopathic physician who might be able to successfully treat this. I thanked them profusely for their help and wished them the best with their new home. Interestingly, within one month of giving us this information, they would move out. Another example of how people show up in our lives for a reason.

This doctor, Dr. Jorge Cochran, turned out to be another huge piece of the puzzle and amazingly enough and by no coincidence he and Dr. Kim had actually shared mutual patients. He suggested doing several tests on the gut, as 90% of the body's neurotransmitters, the chemical messengers responsible for mood, are located in lining of one's gut, hence, why it is often referred to as the "second brain." The tests revealed Tim's gut was almost completely devoid of the essential neurotransmitters such as dopamine, serotonin, GABA, etc. Again, although it's difficult to get results such as these that show a problem, it did provide relief in that it gave us another specific diagnosis. Dr. Cochran believed the mold and thyroid issues, along with potential damage from past antibiotic use, foreign bacteria and viruses from international travel, and poor food choices throughout his life, had destroyed his gut and left him with a compromised intestinal tract – sometimes called leaky gut syndrome or increased intestinal permeability. The recommendation was to take at least three months off from work while taking several natural and homeopathic supplements to replenish the neurotransmitters and allow the gut to heal. Tim was also instructed to work with a nutritionist who specialized in rebuilding the gut through specialized and restrictive diets (i.e. using food as medicine).

This extremely personal experience with my husband's chronic illness coupled with my professional experience as a therapist continues to shed light on the complexities of how we treat and heal illness. There are many more people out there then we may realize struggling for years with multi-faceted complex illness, yet what percentage of these illnesses are strictly medical? There are always emotional dimensions to and of a medical illness possibly brought on by past traumas, chronic stress and life-changing events that have been stuffed in the body and ignored until the body gets our attention in such a way that we are forced to face it. So for Tim, this was not only a journey of treating the medical conditions but also an opportunity for him to move forward in life by recognizing, confronting, and embracing the life-changing events from his past that were not only contributing to his medical condition but serving as stumbling blocks for his recovery.

At the time of this writing, I am proud and blessed to say my husband has made a strong recovery and has taken the lessons he has learned from this illness and integrated them into the work he has been doing. He has been back working with youth in the classroom and in the workforce development field for close to three years now and has been heavily involved with a national mentoring organization that provides adolescent boys emotional guidance and support on their journey to manhood. As much as we celebrate his recovery, the physical, mental, and emotional toll it took on me is still working itself out. However, both he and I have found tremendous healing through working on this book together. So although my life was "interrupted" for many years, this ordeal has left both of us with gifts and lessons that have allowed us to grow personally, professionally, and as a couple.

Throughout any challenging situation, there are always messages and opportunities for personal growth, if we choose to be open to them. This arduously long four-year battle with Tim's chronic illness tore down every foundation of the life we had built together and tested the strength of our commitment to each other in countless ways as our roles changed from co-equal partners to one of dependency and caregiving. For me, although most people around me saw me as a very strong, spiritual female, I hadn't yet begun to scratch the surface of how much strength, courage, and tenacity I truly had. One of the key lessons for me on this journey and throughout my life has been to lean even more heavily on my spiritual side – my angels, guides, helpers, the Divine, and the messages from those on the other side who had transitioned – particularly when some of those whom I expected and hoped would show up for support didn't. I was forced to look deeper within myself and outside of this earthly realm for the support I needed.

And through it all, this ordeal has left me in a much better position to work with my clients as the medical research and experience I gained gave me a wide range of information and personal experience to help them through a variety of health-related issues that have interconnected medical, mental, emotional, and spiritual components. I have been able to integrate much of this information into the work I do with my clients, which has truly been a blessing – a theme I will expand on in subsequent chapters.

As Tim started getting healthier, I had to learn to pull back from my caregiver role and give him the space to continue his healing journey on his own. I had to trust he would continue to stay healthy by taking ownership of the healing process and had learned to connect to his body on his own. I also had to trust he would be able to identify the emotions his body had been holding for him before, during, and after the illness as this was a significant piece of the healing puzzle.

In turn, he would tell me just how much he has learned through this process about what 'support' truly looks like. Although it began back in Virginia, his understanding crystallized the moment I broke down after his brother's phone call when he truly began to realize just how much I had carried for him, and for us. From this point we have been able to grow closer as a couple in ways that would never have been possible before. From the moment Tim uttered those intentions to the universe at a sweat lodge in Maya Tulum, he has been on a journey of learning how to step into a new role of being a better husband, a best friend, and a support system for me. By forcing us out of our comfort zone in Virginia and leading us to a place where we had no friends, family, or support systems, we have been divinely-led to rebuild our lives and learn to rely on each other. As we both have learned who we are and what we're made of, this has helped us discover who we are as a couple and how we can best support each other. This, to me, is the essence of finding meaning through traumatic situations. This is the "gift" we have received through the challenge.

8

A HUSBAND'S CLARITY

"Letting go is a spiritual, emotional, mental & physical process, a mysterious metaphysical process of releasing to God and the universe that which we are clinging to so tightly. There is magic in letting go."

~ Melody Beattie, "The Language of Letting Go"

Helping my wife edit the chapter "Life Interrupted" and seeing those words in print was beyond difficult for me. I can't tell you how many emotions it tapped into and brought up as I had to relive one of the most excruciatingly painful periods of my life. It is one thing to talk about it but quite another to see it in print. It's like the event is crystallized. And given the personal nature of how it happened, what she and I both went through, and the toll it took on both of us, especially my wife, was completely devastating.

I felt compelled to write this chapter for several reasons. First and foremost, I wanted to support my wife and validate the work she did for me in terms of carrying the financial burden and providing unmeasurable emotional support and sacrifice. Secondly, I write this as living proof of what her unique healing approach can do and how the different therapeutic methods she exposed me to can be beneficial. I should emphasize the significance of this as a left-brained, Western-mindset, evidence-based skeptic of anything smacking of the term 'alternative' or 'holistic.' This was a completely new world for me as I was raised to place the locus of control outside of myself in the form of medical providers who knew more about my body than I did. This is in no way meant to discount the knowledge and expertise medical providers bring but seeing that they are trained in the 'art of medicine,' I now believe patients have to take some degree of ownership for their own healing and become part of the equation so as to allow medical providers to better perform their art. We need to trust in our own inner knowing, use our intuition, research multiple options, ask as many questions as we can from friends, family, and others who might have experienced what we are going through, and use a broad array of information, including doctor's advice, to make the most informed decision that works for us. My wife's central message about getting in touch with your own body and learning to trust in its wisdom was something completely foreign to me but it would be a lesson I learned well, albeit the hard way.

This is one of the lessons I learned through my battle with chronic illness. Not only did I learn how to get in touch with my body and trust my instincts but I learned how to be an advocate for myself as I watched my wife be the strongest advocate you can possibly imagine. So many times I was asked why I wouldn't go the extra distance for myself in the same way I would for the kids I worked with. Good point. This was something I had to learn through my medical illness as one of my life themes has become learning to speak up and advocate for myself.

Another lesson I learned through this battle is that every illness and/or disease has an emotional component. As my wife has championed this concept with her clients, the emotional toll this illness took not just on me but on her as well became steadfast validation. For me, I had stuffed my emotions down since the seventh grade. The adolescent years of growing up in school can be one of the most difficult times in a person's life. Simply trying to 'fit in' and 'be cool' is hard enough to contend with but add to it the potential of peer pressure, rejection, social cliques, bullying, and all sorts of societal and parental expectations during a time when hormones are running wild and you have the perfect recipe for emotional turmoil. I was no exception, as I would venture to guess every other kid goes through the same struggles. No one is immune.

Although I thought I was one of the fortunate ones to escape adolescence by being relatively well-liked, enjoyed a degree of athletic achievement and recognition, and found meaning and purpose through academic success, my formula for "success" was to push down my emotions and never let "feelings" get in the way. I ploughed through life as a "doer" – something I'm sure most males can relate to as society reinforces this role. My choice then was to block my emotions and stuff them down to avoid any pain. It's a great survival mechanism but after thirty-five years of stuffing down emotions, there comes a time when the body simply can't take it anymore. At some point, these bottled-up emotions have to find a way out. So to get your attention, they bubble up through illness or disease.

In my case, they came out through a four-year battle with an illness that challenged every aspect of my daily functioning. It took away almost everything I had going for me. It took away my ability to concentrate and focus, making life at work almost as scary and frightening as you can imagine. Having graduated from college, achieving two master's degrees, living overseas in the Middle East (during September 11, 2001), and working in very demanding professions (i.e. teaching) and not being able to write an email or comprehend what I was reading was beyond difficult. My energy was taken away to the point where I had to give up many of the recreational activities I had always loved to do, most notably coaching baseball. My relationship with my wife would be put to the most unbearable test as our home was taken away and we moved across the country where we had no friends, family, or support system. Not to mention I didn't have a job so I would have to restart my career once I became healthy. The challenge was immense.

Up until the spring of 2011, I considered myself to be a pretty healthy guy. I worked in public and charter schools throughout Virginia, Maryland, and D.C. and barely took a sick day. All that changed in the spring of 2011 when a mysterious illness brought me to my knees; literally and figuratively. The symptoms have been described already but what I can say is that my world was being systematically torn down. My most valuable commodity – my energy – was stripped from me. I was about as active as you can get coaching baseball, riding bikes, hiking, playing golf, and going for daily/nightly walks with my wife. This all came crashing down that spring as by mid-March I could hardly walk around the block without collapsing in fatigue.

Worse than my physical health, my mental health was taken away from me. I would wake up in the morning feeling "off." It's hard to explain but I just wasn't my usual, confident self. I became very anxious and worried and struggled to face the day. Simple, mundane, ordinary tasks that I used to carry out in my sleep such as reading, responding to emails, and being present and productive during meetings at work became overwhelming. All I wanted to do was stay in bed and hide. It sounds like depression but I can tell you it was something much worse. I had no idea what was happening to me but it scared the hell out of me because I began to feel as though I wouldn't be able to function in this world the way I used to and the way I wanted to.

This was by far one of the scariest times in my life. I had no idea what was happening to me but I did have an incredible support system. My family was always there for me offering support throughout as were my good friends that kept tabs and continually checked-in on me. But most of all I had a wife whose tenacity and unwavering (and I mean unwavering) support could be matched by no one. From the minute I broke down some time in mid-February and shared with her my fear of the strange symptoms that were starting to envelope me, she took it upon herself to not only find the best medical treatment but also find the root cause of this illness – something that felt like a Gordian Knot.

You're probably sick of hearing about the physical, mental, emotional, energetic, nutritional, and spiritual components by this point but I'm going to include them anyway not only because they are important but because it shows how she transformed this left-brained, analytical, Western, evidence-based guy into a believer of how integrative care and alternative therapies from a holistic perspective can contribute to the healing process. Upon reflection, there's no coincidence as to why I went through what I did. As difficult as it was for me, it was a way, a rather hard way, of really learning what it is about my wife's work that aids in the healing process for her clients. I believe the only way I would have been able to truly understand this is by going through it myself and really feeling what it was like. Interesting way of looking at it, eh?

My illness taught me a great many things. For me, I will never again take my health for granted. I had been relatively healthy up until that point but this experience opened my eyes as to just how delicate and fragile our health can be. Interestingly, as sick as I was, it gave me the opportunity to appreciate just how lucky I was not to have an even more severe illness. The process of filling out endless patient health forms that list every disease under the sun and being able to check "No" next to most boxes actually served to lift my spirits. I guess in some strange way knowing how much worse you can be from a relative standpoint can be liberating and reassuring. Despite the fact that I had no energy, was anxious, confused, and overwhelmed with normal stimuli, and had an impending sense of dread that things wouldn't improve, at least I didn't have some of the major life-threatening diseases. So a positive takeaway was the reassurance that I wasn't as bad off as others. But this reassurance quickly wore off as soon as I left the medical facility and saw people fully engaged in life and work – an immediate reminder of where I was not. So the roller coaster of what had now become my life continued.

The hardest part of this illness was the ambiguity and lack of a clear, definable diagnosis. As my wife mentioned in the Life Interrupted chapter, we felt like we were swimming in "unchartered waters." Might be fun for an explorer or an adventure-seeker but when you have a medical condition that's threatening everything you stood for personally, professionally, and recreationally, swimming in uncertainty is not a fun place to be. As human beings, it's comforting when we're able to identify the root cause of a problem (i.e. medical diagnosis). This gives us an identifiable goal and a blueprint for treatment, as well as reassurance that others have gone down this path and have recovered. The most important part of this is it gives the patient a feeling of control – something I sorely wanted and needed but did not have. When someone breaks a leg, there is an X-ray, a diagnosis, and an evidence-based course of treatment. Although I'm sure this is an unpleasant situation and a very painful one at that, there is comfort in having the peace of mind of having a good idea as to how the process of recovery will work. Timelines certainly help as we can plan and anticipate when we'll be back on our feet, no pun intended, and be back at work. In my case, I had no such luck.

The difficulty now lay in the fact that I was being treated for an illness that wasn't fully accepted in the world of Western medicine. Although there is plenty of research and countless case studies of folks getting sick from mold, this type of neurotoxin illness had yet to be accepted by one of the most important parts of the health care industry – insurance companies. Despite a twenty-six page document I submitted to my insurance company to receive short-term disability benefits, that included mold test results, remediation verification, letters from my integrative doctors describing the mold illness protocol I was being given, and countless lab tests and bloodwork, I was denied. You can imagine the financial burden this placed on my wife as she continued working two jobs to make ends meet. And here I was sitting at home feeling guilty for not being able to contribute. A horrible place to be.

I share this to help create context for the psychological stress I was under and how I'm sure it contributed to prolonging and making my recovery more difficult. And just when we thought we were in the clear when we moved to Tucson, my symptoms reared their ugly heads yet again and gave me that final leg to get over. As a baseball player, this seemed like strike three to me. I didn't think I was going to get out of this one. The mold was left behind and we were in a new, dry, mold-free climate but something hadn't cleared up in me. This is when we found another excellent doctor, a Naturopathic MD, who recognized my gut had been destroyed for a number of reasons and the answer lay in cleaning it up and rebuilding it.

Eventually my gut did repair itself through a restrictive diet and several supplements designed to boost my gut's production of neurotransmitters – the chemical messengers responsible for moods and how we feel. I eased back into work several months later by taking my licks in the classroom as a substitute teacher before landing a full-time teaching job that would morph into my current position where I work at helping at-risk youth make successful transitions to the workforce through education and training programs. In many ways, the work I do mirrors the transition I had to make myself through my recovery process. Not only did I have to rebuild myself mentally and physically but had to rebuild my professional career by working my way from an entry-level standpoint – something that can be very challenging on a lot of levels, especially in a new environment, not to mention on the psyche.

As a direct consequence of this illness, not only have I become a stronger person but have been able to relate with my students and the youth I work with on much deeper levels as I now can better understand and appreciate the challenges and struggles they face. I make sure my curriculum and the programs I help design incorporate a trauma-informed care approach and bring a level of compassion for the individual that was not there before my illness. I also work to dispel the myth that talking about feelings and emotions, particularly for males, is weak. In fact, I believe it's exactly the opposite. I know there is a very strong stigma against seeking counseling and/or therapy for males, particularly in this country, but I am not the least bit ashamed to admit having utilized these types of treatments in my recovery process. I was fortunate to find therapists who had gone through life-changing illnesses themselves and could relate to the process I was going through.

As I alluded to in the opening quote for this chapter, there is something quite liberating about physically getting your feelings and emotions out. This is a message I share with the youth I work with as my role often times serves as a de facto counselor, mentor, and even pseudo-parent. This is also why I have become involved with several mentoring organizations, including a national organization with a local chapter here in Tucson, that provides opportunities for boys to share their experiences, feelings, and struggles in school-based and extracurricular settings as we, adult mentors, support them on their journey to manhood. I believe we need to tear down the stigma that attaches negative connotations to seeking help and views sharing and talking about feelings as being weak. It is time to recognize and support the social and emotional growth of our youth, particularly our young males.

More importantly it has helped bring me much closer to my wife in ways that wouldn't have been possible before the illness. Just like Infinity, my pet ball python who started out as a classroom pet but now occupies a space in our home, I had to 'shed my skin' so to speak and literally go through a process of rebirth – something I don't think is uncommon. Watching Paige write this book and helping her edit the chapters, particularly Life Interrupted, has reinforced the many lessons I learned from the challenge and has brought us closer in ways that we would never have imagined. I see it as no coincidence that my struggle in finding meaning through my illness served to help me appreciate and understand and truly get what she does so I could help her articulate her message for the world. Coincidence? I think not.

"Life has meaning only in the struggle.
Triumph or defeat is in the hands of God.
So let us celebrate the struggle."

~ Swahili War Song
Featured in the movie "Lorenzo's Oil"

9

THE JOURNEY OF CAREGIVING

Sitting in my car with the top down looking out onto the Potomac River from the George Washington Parkway while crying uncontrollably had become one of my weekly self-care routines. As I sat there bundled up in my winter hat, gloves, and scarf with the seat warmer on high, I would listen to the comforting song Blessings by Laura Story and reflect on just how much my life had changed with my husband's illness.

Being a caregiver for someone you love can be one of the most challenging roles you can experience in this lifetime. You and your loved one's life, along with your goals, dreams, and passions will most likely have to be put on hold, or worse yet, never realized as they take a back seat to the immediate needs of your loved one. The experience can be about as emotionally taxing as it gets as the added responsibility of having to make life and death decisions can weigh on the body and mind, not to mention the anxiety and fear it can create when these decisions conflict with the choices others, especially family members, would have made. You will second guess yourself, you will wonder how much longer you can hold on, and you will have times of doubt while questioning why this situation is happening. The stress of dealing with all of this can bleed out into all areas of your life and leave you feeling lonely, isolated, and at times depressed.

However, just as your life might seem or feel like it's out of control, you will also be given a wonderful opportunity for self-growth. It will help you deepen your understanding of what's most important in your life and might give you the opportunity to strengthen the bond you have with the one you are caring for. It might also give you an opening to trust in something bigger than yourself outside this earthly realm, as messages will present themselves to teach you how to navigate through this challenging situation. Being open to this bigger picture during this challenging time will help when it feels like you have no answers as to why this is occurring.

It has been my experience both personally and professionally that the role of caregiving will tax you physically, mentally, emotionally, energetically, and spiritually. This is very important to understand because what I have found is that most caregivers get so wrapped up in their new role, they forget to take care of the most important person – themselves. This can easily lead to stress, burnout, depletion, and strong feelings of resentment towards the one you love, not to mention the possibility of medical issues for the caregivers themselves. They don't give themselves permission to be "cared for" even though they are taking care of the needs of others. Often there are feelings of selfishness and guilt for taking time away to do something for themselves. So let me state this clearly and loudly: YOU HAVE FULL PERMISSION TO TAKE CARE OF YOURSELF!!! Think about the example of being on a plane when the oxygen masks come down. You are told to put your mask on first before you help others. It is no different in the world of caregiving. If anything it is more important.

Practicing self-care through this journey is a must! It doesn't have to be expensive but it must be scheduled into your daily life in the same way you would schedule a medical appointment for the one you are caring for. I always advise creating a healing approach that includes self-care you can do on your own while also building a healing team for support. The approach can include anything from taking a walk, sitting in nature, a bath, meditation, yoga, journaling, a brief power nap, exercise, car ride, massage, listening to music, or any other type of activity that allows you to take your mind off caregiving and nourishes your body and soul. I can't tell you how many times I needed to sit in a bathtub as the water was calming, soothing and releasing. It was a place for me to melt into calm and not worry about anyone or anything. This was something I did along with yoga, meditation, prayer and walks.

I also created a healing team for myself which included my integrative doctor, energy body worker, and an integrative therapist. You must remember that in order to be the best you can be for another, you must first be the best you can be for yourself. Sometimes this may mean being vulnerable and asking for help so that you may give yourself a break. I have also found that some caregivers tend to focus exclusively on the person they are caring for which makes it easier for them to ignore, avoid and hide from their own issues and emotions. The only thing this will do is prolong the inevitable of facing and embracing yourself. What you resist, will persist!

Self-care becomes even more important when we think about how the caregiving situation has the potential to create extreme emotional trauma in the body. Remember trauma lodges in the body and can remain even down to a cellular level, especially if there are any unresolved issues from traumatic events or medical illness the caregiver might have had prior to this new role. It is normal to have stress reactions both during and after your caregiving role has completed. Going one step further, even though I don't know of any definitive research, I believe a correlation can be drawn between a long-term caregiving role and post-traumatic stress disorder (PTSD). As with PTSD, a caregiver can relive certain disturbing or emotional events experienced through this situation. They might avoid situations, places, or certain people that remind them of their time as a caregiver and may experience negative changes in their beliefs and feelings towards others. Lastly, caregivers might find themselves having a hard time sleeping, concentrating or focusing. The long-term effects of the physical, emotional, mental and possibly financial stress, as well as the presence of grief, is real and should be given more attention in order to reduce the burden on the caregiver population.

There are many other aspects to the caregiving role but one area I find rarely discussed is how the dynamics of the relationship prior to the illness affect the current situation and add an extra layer of complexity. Although often overlooked, this dynamic is extremely important to understand as it will affect every aspect of the caregiving role from the communication and verbiage you use with your loved one to the way it affects every aspect of your life moving forward. With any relationship there are struggles, challenges, and a plethora of emotions that have transpired from events and situations long before an illness has arisen. Whatever unresolved issues or emotions that didn't get discussed or rectified between the two of you before the illness, will bleed out and get magnified through the caregiver-patient dynamic. Therefore being able to recognize and identify if the emotions you are feeling stem from the caregiving role or from unresolved feelings from the past will be crucial in how this situation will affect your relationship.

The unresolved issues from the past play a bigger role than most can imagine and without fully exploring this aspect, feelings of resentment and anger can and will take center stage. This means there will often be times where both of you will need to have uncomfortable conversations to clear the elephant in the room and make space for lighter energy and healing. Many times I have caregivers tell me they don't want to say what is truly on their mind to their loved one for fear of upsetting them or creating undue emotional turmoil. I am here to tell you this is exactly the time and space for you to capitalize on the wonderful opportunity for growth between the two of you. Keeping the emotions and unresolved feelings inside will not only fuel regret, guilt, and anger but will be counterproductive for the healing process. Everything you are feeling has a purpose and a meaning for both yourself and your loved one. Remember, this situation you are experiencing is much bigger than the caregiver-patient role. It is an opportunity for you to view your life and your relationship from a higher perspective and step into the messages of self-growth for you, your loved one, and the relationship, no matter the final outcome.

For those of you caring for someone whose brain function and memory might be diminishing, particularly when caring for those with Alzheimer's, I would like to share with you some insight that will give you some hope and comfort. If your loved one is no longer able to communicate as they once used to, or is incapable of speaking altogether, what I want you to know is communication is still possible on a soul level. The soul is ever present and CAN hear every word you are saying just as Allison was able to take in every word her mother was saying to her during her final moments when she was no longer able to verbally communicate. If you never had a chance to say what you wanted or needed prior to this type of situation, know that you still can..............they WILL hear you.

Another component of this loving yet challenging role is having to deal with the underlying expectations, and often the disappointment, of who does or doesn't show up in this time of need to offer support and assistance. Hopefully all of you will receive support from your family and friends but often times many of us, myself included, are left with confusion and disappointment when those we expected and had hoped would show up for us don't. I feel this is a very important facet to address as it not only can cause great emotional turmoil but the feelings of abandonment can negatively affect or hinder the over-all healing process. From my experience, there are many reasons why those we were counting on don't show up. Obviously, past arguments or conflicts that have kept them stuck in their anger can prevent them from moving beyond and showing up but often times the caregiving situation itself acts as a trigger in their own lives. Maybe they had gone through something similar and feel this is too much to relive. Or maybe they have a conscious or subconscious fear that what you are going through could one day happen in their own life and are too fearful to go there. For whatever reason, it is important not to waste too much energy on this but rather look within yourself and be open to receiving support from people, places, and events beyond the obvious or the familiar. Maybe a piece of your journey is about self-reliance or having to trust in the process or learning to gain support outside of this earthly realm or possibly all of the above. Whatever the reason, begin to pay attention to those who do step in at just the right time to give you what you need. Remember: people support in the ways they know how – let their support fill in the gaps you need.

After the caregiving ends, regardless of whether your loved one makes a full or partial recovery or if he or she transitions, the aftermath of your role will begin to surface. When we go through a traumatic event or an ongoing crisis such as this role, the body is forced to be on guard and feels like it can't soften or let up for fear it won't be prepared for what's around the next corner.

However, when the event concludes and the crisis comes to an end, the body will then feel safe to show signs of fatigue, injury, or even illness. Coupled with the physical responses are the deep layers of emotion that were tucked inside and trickled out here and there throughout the caregiving role. As the intensity of these symptoms and emotions have time and space to show their full depth, it becomes important to embrace and feel them to the fullest. You will be given plenty of time to reflect on who you are and who you've become now that the identity of caregiver has come to an end. This is the time to take in all you have experienced and learned through this challenging yet compassionate and loving process.

Within the depths of this challenge, I believe one of the most important lessons to pack in your red bag is to give yourself permission for self-care both during and after the caregiving role and recognize you were given a divine opportunity for inner growth. It is also a time to get in touch with your inner knowing and to trust that every decision you make through this process truly comes from a place of love and compassion for the highest good. Be open to the messages beyond this earthly realm as they might aid, support, and comfort you during this challenging situation as a reminder that you are not alone. You are right where you are supposed to be at every moment. Embrace it. Trust it. Learn from it and grow from within.

10

SHOULD IS SHIT

How many times have you punished yourself with these words: "I should have...?" The word 'should' for most of us has become an everyday part of our vocabulary, something engrained in our daily lives, but is it useful? Is it working for you? When we think about the connotation of this word and how we use it in our lives, it represents a state of mind in which we don't trust ourselves. If you think about it, it's really a form of self-punishment because rather than trusting in the wisdom and integrity of the original decision and being content in the fact that we made the decision for the highest good, we question ourselves, and by extension our knowing, which keeps us in a perpetual cycle of uncertainty and lack of trust in ourselves. 'Should' takes us out of the present and keeps us stuck in the past.

I invite you to look at this from a different lens. Instead of continually questioning ourselves through the use of this word, let's give ourselves permission to recognize we made the best decision with the information we had under the circumstances we were in. It has been my experience that through the decision-making process, most people come from a place of doing no harm to self or others. Although there are certainly exceptions, rather than questioning or beating ourselves up over the outcome of decisions that were made, let's view them as learning opportunities for our personal growth. And in order to do this, you first have to learn to connect and trust your own inner knowing and wisdom.

How many of you have taken a job when you knew in your heart it wasn't right? Maybe you needed it for the money or possibly the status but deep down inside you knew it didn't align with your passion and ultimately came crashing down. How many of you have entered business partnerships or intimate relationships when every fiber of your being told you it didn't feel right? We overlook or overrule our inner knowing or gut instinct by making excuses and trying to explain away how the ends will justify the means but all this does is lead us back to "I should have."

I have come to understand this process very well as I have had to make extremely difficult decisions throughout my life, particularly when it came to making life or death decisions about my husband's medical care. Caregivers, first responders, and medical practitioners understand this as well as they have to make such decisions on a daily basis. It is easy to get trapped in the "should" mentality when we look at the outcomes and ask ourselves if there is something we could have done differently but the guilt and self-punishment this inflicts on us will only serve to create more trauma within the body. I'm here to tell you that if in that moment you made the decision from a place of love and compassion and with the highest good of not only yourself but the other person in mind, then that is all you can do. Embrace it. Trust it. This doesn't always mean situations will turn out perfectly when you trust your knowing but it does mean you did your part in the process of the bigger picture of life. Instead of punishing yourself through the "shoulds," take the time to look at the deeper message in the outcome and view the situation as an opportunity for personal and spiritual growth.

If looking back you realize you weren't present with yourself and decisions were made from a place of fear or anxiety, rest assured you will be given more opportunities to practice and connect to your inner knowing and wisdom. Remember this:

SHOULD IS SHIT!

11

LAND AND ITS MESSAGES

As my client, Julia, and I set out on a land journey as part of her immersion healing retreat, I explained she would feel a gentle 'pull' from specific parts of nature along the way such as plants, animals, rocks, trees, saguaros, or even paths that might avail themselves. We began the journey in a canyon close to my home in the early morning hours to avoid the scorching noonday Arizona sun. I told her to be open to this 'pull' and trust in the information it gives, as we are intimately connected to nature and it to us. It only took several steps before Julia felt the 'pull' to a certain tree. As I gently urged her to go to the tree and touch it, she began to cry. The tree, in all its expansiveness and splendor, gave Julia a message for her personal growth in the same way the body gives us messages. As Julia would later share with me, "the tree was tall, beautiful, and expanding as its branches spread out to the sky. It told me I could stand tall and express myself and not be so small. I was used to staying small all the time. It was telling me that I was not alone as the tree was a reflection of me. I was allowed to have this same bigness and expansiveness in the world." It now felt okay for her to let the branches of herself be expansive and take up space.

As we continued along this path to our final destination, a medicine wheel designed to connect oneself with the rest of the Universe and assist with a stronger mind, body, spirit connection, Julia then began to feel her own power, beauty, and magnificence. And so began her journey with the healing power of nature…

Throughout this book I have touched on the body's innate power and wisdom to heal, but just as the body provides messages for our personal growth and healing, so, too, does Nature. The land and its animals can be a powerful source of healing if we allow ourselves to be open to its messages in the same way we might allow ourselves to be open to the messages the body provides. If you can imagine the time in our history before modern medicine, human civilizations lived, died, and healed, by honoring that which Mother Nature provided. There was a mutual respect for the land and its animals; something that is being challenged today. But just as I have seen and felt this challenge in my own life and will offer some observations on how we can draw parallels between how we mistreat the land and our bodies, I have been given a gift of being able to see a bigger picture of what the land and its animals can provide for us in terms of our own healing. I have always felt a 'pull' to nature, just like Julia experienced, and have sought to incorporate many different aspects of nature into my healing approach through my studies, particularly Biodynamic Craniosacral Trauma Therapy and shamanic healing, the mentors I have trained and worked under, and above all my own innate wisdom and knowing. Being able to share this bigger picture through several situations I've experienced will hopefully allow you to see how nature is interconnected with us and plays an integral part in one's healing journey.

Have you ever given serious thought to the type of environment or surroundings that make you feel the most calm and peaceful? Most of us have an innate pull to some form of nature, even if we find ourselves living and working in the concrete jungles of urban cities. I'd venture to say most of us know what it is about nature we are drawn to whether it be mountains, water, forest, desert, etc. When I ask my clients what type of environment they envision themselves living in, assuming they are not currently in it, most of them can identify a specific form of nature that draws them in or has that 'pull.' I know for me, I am drawn to water, which might sound contradictory given we live in the desert, but I do believe different forms of nature feed our souls at different times in our lives for different purposes. Growing up on the East Coast and living a few blocks from the Potomac River in Alexandria, Virginia for ten years before moving to Tucson, my 'pull' to the water was certainly being met. But when my husband became ill and I had a chance to visit Tucson shortly thereafter, the magnificent Catalina Mountains spoke very clearly to me saying we needed to relocate to the desert for a time of healing. I believe messages like this come to us, if we are open to them, just as they do through our bodies. This is why I have my clients focus on the aspects of nature that feed them and encourage them to listen to the wisdom of all that nature provides.

As I listened to the message of the Catalina Mountains, I was given signs of validation through nature and beyond. As I mentioned in the 'Life Interrupted' chapter, Archangel Michael left a very visible sign for the two of us in the form of a snow angel when we received the keys to our new home. Another sign came through a plant my grandmother had given me years before she transitioned. When we packed up our belongings to move to Tucson, I packed up my house plants and placed them neatly and safely in a box. The most important of these was a shamrock plant my grandmother had given me which I keep by my bed next to a picture of her. She always told me the shamrocks would close up in the evening to sleep and awaken in the morning. I watered this plant and all the others very heavily before they had to travel in a dark moving van from Alexandria to Tucson for at least five to six days in the middle of winter.

When the moving van arrived at our new home, I began to unpack each box while trying to find the one with the plants. Seeing that many of our things had been thrown around and broken during the trip, it was clear to me this journey had not been an easy one as it mirrored all that was going on in our life. As I opened up the plant box, I found many of the plants with broken limbs and in desperate need of water. At the very bottom of the box, with a heavy brass golden planter that had been jostled during the move on top of it, was the shamrock plant. I can't tell you how nervous I was to check out its condition as I feared it would either be crushed or even worse, dead. Instead, what I found was a plant that had not only grown in size but had bloomed several white flowers. This plant and my grandmother were giving me a clear message that life can still blossom in the dark.

By now you know I have spent time in some places around the world that have witnessed some of the most devastating acts of violence and tragedy. From Ground Zero in New York directly after the terrorist attacks of 9/11 to the war zones of Iraq and the war-torn villages of Rwanda after the genocide, as well as scenes following car accidents, homicides, and suicides, I have seen and felt some of the most tragic events one can possibly imagine. Yet within each of these tragedies where violence, death, trauma, and hatred lurked, I also paradoxically found hope, healing and angelic support. When I try to explain this, most people find it hard to comprehend, let alone understand, how these opposing forces and feelings can co-exist in the same space at the same time. As difficult as it is to explain, what I can say is that I am able to feel the energies of both sides as they are supported by the land. The land serves as the foundation, or placeholder if you will. Just as Holden Caulfield envisions himself as the 'catcher in the rye' where he catches wayward youth from falling over the cliff of a wheat field, the land serves to catch the energy of the violent act or natural disaster. The visible part to most human beings is the violence or the violent act itself and those who show up to support both during and after the event such as first responders, good Samaritans, and anyone who lovingly assists in the devastation. There is another side to these tragedies that I am able to sense and feel which is not visible to most human beings. I am able to see and feel certain souls who transitioned in the tragedy who have presented themselves to me. At the same time I am able to connect, hear, and feel the light beings and angelic support from beyond this earthly realm who show up as well to offer support. They, too, come to these particular places where the land is holding the energy of the event. To better understand this paradox let me share with you a few experiences where the visible and the angelic support co-exist on the land.

While visiting the country of Rwanda as part of a group of subject matter experts in PTSD with a People-to-People delegation organized to assist local officials with developing systemic responses to the recovery of the genocide, I was given a strong message during a visit to a local church. As part of our mission, we were taken to various sites throughout the country, particularly those most affected by the genocide, to give us a better understanding of the devastation and toll it took on the population and country as a whole. One of the sites we visited was a local church which had been the scene of a brutal massacre involving many children who had been in attendance when the killing spree began. I distinctly remember walking into the church and seeing remnants of the clothes they had been wearing laid out as a memorial and as a reminder of the devastation and brutality. As we walked through the church, a bright multi-colored wave of light spread over the children's clothing and I could sense the movement of souls dancing in and out of the light. I turned to one of my colleagues and asked if she was seeing the same thing but she was not. In fact, none of my colleagues acknowledged seeing the bright light as I described. When I reflect back on this experience, it is clear to me the land was holding the violence of the massacre, yet at the same time it was holding the joy and laughter of the children from the other side. The message I received was that these children, although brutally murdered from the visible part of this human existence, were experiencing no pain or suffering in the afterlife, instead joy and lightness prevailed. Their angelic presence was analogous to the messages I had received from other souls who were 'pulled out' prior to violent and traumatic deaths. This in no way should be interpreted as condoning the violence but rather a reassurance of hope that peace and comfort can be found in the afterlife as souls never die.

Another place where I felt the land holding messages was Ground Zero in New York. Following my work assisting victims of the terrorist attack, I traveled back to New York to attend the first anniversary of the event. As I walked around the grounds, I could feel many of the souls of those who had transitioned in the attack moving around in a funnel-like swirling fashion enveloping all of us who were standing on the land. I could hear and feel their messages of support, hope, protection, and comfort. A decade later while the One World Trade Center was being constructed, Hurricane Sandy, one of the deadliest and most destructive hurricanes of 2012, hit the East coast with a vengeance. That evening while I was meditating and sending out prayers to all who were in the storm's path, I was shown an image of the cranes sitting on top of the building that were being used for its construction. I had great concern for their stability and feared they might collapse under the force of the hurricane causing destruction to an area that couldn't handle any more pain. However the message I was given was that the land underneath the crane, which was still holding the energy of the terrorist attack and now the energy of the crane, was gaining support from beyond this earthly realm. The support came from three souls who had perished in the attack along with other light beings who were on top of the crane holding it in place until the hurricane passed. As it came to be, the cranes miraculously survived the hurricane-force winds from Superstorm Sandy.

In the summer of 2015, my husband and I, along with his parents, took a two-week road trip vacation through several parts of Arizona and Colorado. On our final leg of the journey, which included stops in Sedona, Durango, the Grand Canyon, and Winslow (*to see the famous 'corner' immortalized by the Eagles), we stopped to see one of Arizona's most spectacular geologic formations. Horseshoe Bend in the Glen Canyon National Recreation Area is a horseshoe-shaped meander of the Colorado River with a scenic view that brings tourists from far and wide. There is a good forty-five minute walk from the parking lot along a sandy trail amidst a backdrop of the stunning Arizona red rock. Little did I know that I would soon receive messages that would take my intuitive and clairvoyant gifts to a new dimension.

As we were walking back from the site after taking the obligatory round of tourist photos, I was suddenly stopped in my tracks from messages that were coming up from the land underneath my feet. I motioned for my husband and in-laws to keep moving ahead while I remained transfixed in this one particular area. What I felt and heard beneath my feet were female voices telling me they were trapped as they did not know how to release themselves from the land. I'm not sure of the history of this particular piece of land but I have to assume something violent, possibly a battle, had taken place there. As tourists poured past me in droves, I tried to look as inconspicuous as possible as I worked on releasing them from the land. I had released other stuck souls before but never from the land in this manner. As I stood upon the land in the intuitive way I knew how, I was able to release and allow these souls to move forward on their next journey. As I have spoken with other individuals like me who have similar yet different gifts, we often share experiences like these that continue to awe and amaze us. Each one of us is contacted differently by souls and we each use our own unique gifts in assisting them on their journey.

In closing, I would like to draw some parallels between the treatment of the land and our bodies. In the beginning of this chapter I mentioned how I felt the mutual respect for the land and its animals is being challenged in this day and age. I also mentioned how the land holds messages in the same way our bodies hold our life stories. In the same way we pollute, destroy, and harm the land through overdevelopment, use of toxic chemicals, and exploitation of natural resources, we do the same to our bodies. We do this by pushing our bodies beyond its limits and letting our brains and egos dictate what the body wants instead of letting the body tell us what it needs. Our current lifestyles often involve eating and drinking unhealthy foods and drinks, ingesting toxic chemicals from everyday products, and leave little down time for rest, recovery, and nurturing of the body and soul. When we continue to avoid, neglect, push and exploit the body in these ways, these negative actions become reflected back to us through illness, injury, and disease just as the land and its animals reflect back to us depletion, exhaustion of resources, toxicity, and lack of life. This creates unsustainability in both the land and our bodies. Although some might disagree, there is a growing body of research-based, scientific evidence to suggest the land is pushing back through climate change and other indicators of environmental harm. I believe it is important to recognize how nature is using these signs to get our attention in the same way we might recognize how the body gives us signs for our own healing.

This begins with gaining a deeper appreciation of all the land has to offer. When I take people out on the land for journeying, they are re-connecting to a nurturing and life-giving source that offers support and messages without judgement. They begin to listen in a new way and view the land and its animals from a different lens. They become more aware of how these things carry messages for their current life circumstances. As all of us are intimately connected to every other living system on this planet through a universal life force of energy and vibration, re-connecting with nature will help strengthen your connection to the healing power of your inner wisdom and knowing.

12

THE MISSING LINK

Throughout this book I have shared stories and personal examples of my experiences with topics such as life, death, trauma, caregiving, and finding meaning in challenging situations. I have shared these to assist you on your own personal healing journey and to let you know that you are not alone on this journey. This brings me to the core of my personal approach – tapping into the innate power and wisdom of the body and using the assistance that is there for us beyond this earthly realm. My hope for you is that by sharing my overall healing approach and how it has helped others, particularly the following three individuals who were courageous enough to share their stories in the interest of helping others and paying it forward, you may see yourself or someone you love in these examples which will hopefully help as a reminder that you are not alone and that meaning, purpose, and healing can be found.

As someone who has experienced many levels of trauma, which I believe contributed to many of the medical conditions I've had to deal with throughout my life, it became very natural for me to disconnect from my physical body. What I realized and understood through my own journey of healing was that my body held the stories and messages from the trauma and the medical conditions it had endured. As I started to listen and work with my body's innate wisdom, there was a profound shift in the way I was able to deal with the trauma, which subsequently led to improvement with the medical conditions I had been battling. Therefore, I began to use and hone this approach on the clients I worked with who came from a variety of backgrounds and brought levels of trauma and medical issues from the conditions they had been exposed to as well. The clients included various populations such as men, women and children of all ages, first responders (law enforcement, fire/EMS), military, Special Forces, refugees, LGBT and transgender, those who are medically and terminally ill, and practitioners in the health and wellness field. As I found tremendous success helping them mend from a place of fracturing back to a state of wholeness by re-connecting them to their bodies, it became clear to me that a 'missing link' in our current health and wellness system is utilizing the body's own innate wisdom and power to heal. This core belief serves as the foundation of my healing approach.

This gentle, non-invasive approach allows clients to get into their bodies and receive the information it is holding for their healing. Your body holds every second of every moment you've experienced in this lifetime whether it brought you joy, love, confidence, panic, fear, grief and every emotion in between. Your life story lives and breathes inside your bodily fluids, organs, glands, nerve cells, sensory systems and musculoskeletal system. Often times the most difficult and challenging stories the body holds are the ones that wreak the most havoc in our lives. These stories, when stuffed, denied, and minimized, will often show themselves through injury, illness, and disease as a way of getting our attention. Even then, many people will continue to ignore, deny, and push the body without honoring the messages it is trying to give to them for their healing. As human beings we use our brain to tell the body what it is going to do, how it is going to do it, and the length of time it will do it for, without ever giving the body permission to speak its truth. I help my clients interpret, understand, and ultimately embrace the information these messages are giving them. They begin to decipher the difference between the true and authentic messages the body holds as opposed to the often misleading information the brain and ego give which might serve to keep them stuck by perpetuating the old patterns of behavior and old ways of thinking.

Since the core of my approach centers around learning to trust one's own innate wisdom or knowing, you may be asking yourself what does that really mean? Trying to explain one's knowing is like trying to explain the color blue to a blind person who has never been able to see. It's hard to explain but you just know the color blue because at some point in your life you were taught the colors of the color wheel. Our knowing is something deep down inside all of us, something deeper than instincts. It is an internal guidance system or an internal compass that allows us to navigate our daily course through this life. I teach my clients how to hear and sense this, how to feel it, and ultimately how to trust it. And when they do learn how to trust their knowing, it opens up a powerful source of healing and wisdom that helps in every facet of their lives whether it be personal relationships, career, health, wellness, and beyond. This power comes from being able to place themselves at the center of their own healing - an empowering process that runs contrary to the patient being a passive observer in his or her own healing by placing the power in the hands of external sources.

This was the case with my client Erin, who was able to find the center of her own healing after surviving one of the most horrific traffic accidents the state of New York has ever witnessed. Erin was a 17-year-old ice hockey star from Vancouver whose life was turned literally upside down when her team's coach bus veered off the interstate and smashed head-on into a parked tractor trailer at a speed of 70mph, leaving the bus impaled on the back of the rig. When Erin was taken by ambulance to the hospital, she found her father waiting for her as he had been at the hotel room at the time of the accident. Since she and her mother had been sitting separately on the bus, she and her father anxiously awaited word of her mother's condition. As friends and family gathered at the hospital to re-unite with the injured team members, Erin and her father never imagined what the Sheriff was about to tell them. The crash had left three people dead: Erin's coach and his 13-year-old son and Erin's mother who happened to be sitting close to the front of the bus upon impact. As evening turned to morning, the accident had been plastered on the front page of every local newspaper with a picture of someone carrying a body bag. Erin knew it was her mother.

Erin, herself, was critically injured, as were many other people on the bus. Her physical injuries included severe whiplash, bruising from the collarbone to the elbow, and hip impingement, as well as a case of TMJ so severe her teeth began to die and fall out. She was also diagnosed with ADHD from the impact of the trauma on her brain and suffered from short-term memory loss. She had difficulty focusing and concentrating and struggled for years to fully process and comprehend written and verbal communication. The trauma of the accident along with the emotional, mental, and physical pain she had to endure as a result left her almost incapable of functioning on a daily basis.

For the next two years Erin was completely numb and could not even remember who she was prior to the accident. She does remember being very angry and taking this anger out on others around her, particularly her father. Her life situation was beyond challenging as her father wasn't able to comfort or be present for her in the way her mother had been able to do. With her life spiraling out of control, she began controlling some of the things which she could: exercise and eating habits. Outwardly, she pretended to be fine but this was simply masking the intense stages of grief, guilt, and anger she was experiencing deep down inside.

For seven years Erin fought and struggled through life as classic signs and symptoms of PTSD would manifest. She struggled daily with flashbacks, nightmares, frightening thoughts, avoidant behaviors, strong guilt, depression, constant tension and worry, difficulty sleeping, and suffered angry outbursts that at times seemed uncontrollable. At one point she cut herself off from the world and became a hermit as the ongoing court trials of reliving the accident and losing her mom consumed and crippled her with severe emotional pain.

In October of 2012 while visiting her boyfriend's family in Washington, D.C., she came across my website while looking for a practitioner. After contacting me and learning about my healing approach, as well as the extensive experience I had with trauma, she made an appointment. What I found in my office that day was a strong, beautiful, determined, yet fragile, woman who was unbelievably broken after having been forced to suffer more trauma than anyone can be expected to handle. I could tell her self-confidence was extremely low and her sense of self had been fractured. As such, I gently helped her become reacquainted with a body she had become disconnected from years ago.

As she learned how to ground and re-connect to her body, she began to find the answers to her own questions regarding the horrible accident and how it had been affecting her physically, emotionally, mentally, energetically, medically, nutritionally and spiritually. I knew that an important part of her deep healing would be the need to re-connect with her mother in the afterlife, which I helped her do using my mystical gifts. This enabled her to share with her mother the deep feelings of guilt she carried for not being able to help her and even for surviving the accident. Equally imperative for her emotional healing was that she learned through this communication that her mother's soul had been pulled out long before the impact of the crash and had been at Erin's side ensuring she would live through the horrible tragedy.

Soon after we began working together, Erin felt less on edge and was able to get a deeper night's sleep. We worked on using her voice to speak her authentic truth, which gave her the confidence to begin articulating her thoughts in a coherent way that wasn't as scattered and disjointed as before. I had her connect to her emotions through her body without fear, allowing her to feel and understand them in all their pain, anguish, and misery. She was then able to release, rewire and let them go, which freed her up to begin living her life again. We worked on staying present in the moment and releasing the need to detach from the body when situations became stressful as her body was there to speak to her, giving her insight always. Erin learned that she didn't have to continually punish herself anymore for what she couldn't control that fateful day. She was able to return to those things she loved such as painting, writing, hiking and began to see the great potential she had in herself to help others on their journey. This also helped her open up and connect with her boyfriend at the time who would one day become her husband. As a result, Erin is now happily married, owns a CrossFit Gym with her husband, is currently in school to obtain a nutritional certification and has a renewed sense of purpose. As I interviewed her for this book, she shared with me that she is "always changing and growing, allowing my soul to experience it all as it is never ending. I'm not afraid to find out what else life has in store for me. I'm stepping into and becoming who I am supposed to be. I'm in a very good place."

As Erin experienced a traumatic and life-altering event with the accident, another one of my clients lived daily in a world of trauma, with the extraordinary juxtaposition of being tasked to save lives while having to take others.

Sean, whose name has been changed for privacy reasons, was a 48-year-old Special Forces medic with additional assaulter/sniper duties who flew out to Arizona to see me for an intense, three-day immersion retreat. I was recommended to him by a mutual friend who had worked with me for years and knew my expertise in working with Special Forces, military, law enforcement, and the first responder population. I've always had tremendous respect for the men and women who put their lives on the line to protect us and keep our communities and country safe. Having worked with first responder populations for years at the Pentagon, Arlington County [VA], and in Iraq, I understand the daily challenges they face and the psychological mindset that goes along with the profession. I also believe the best way to serve these populations is to be able to put oneself in their shoes to really understand what the job is like. In order to do this and better understand the physical and mental demands the profession places them under, I have worked alongside law enforcement professionals by arriving on-scene for domestics, suicides, and homicides, and have participated in many ride-alongs with police, fire and medics. I have also participated in live burns with the Arlington County Fire Department, worked in the war zones of Iraq and have cross-trained with S.W.A.T. teams on tactical measures. Having these experiences and this level of understanding was a critical piece in building that first layer of trust with Sean, especially as I was able to relate to the tricky dynamic he had to balance between having to function one minute as a combatant performing assaulter/sniper duties and then having to flip the switch the next minute to handling medic duties. My time on the front lines with first responders and in combat zones became critical for serving Sean and this population.

Sean came to see me for several reasons. He explained that he was "totally tapped out with no reserves left." He had been running flat out while in service and took the same work ethic into civilian life. He was frustrated with the total lack of focus and strategic planning of corporate business. He was also frustrated with the lack of help from the Veteran Administration (VA) but most of all he was grieving over the fact that he couldn't save everyone that he had treated and friends were still dying on deployments. As a medic with assaulter/sniper duties in the Special Forces, Sean explained that he had some good successes and was able to save some severely injured teammates. Eventually though, he explained that he was humbled by not being able to save a teammate while involved in an engagement, which continues to haunt him even with the fundamental understanding that this is combat. As he states, "Medical providers will always second guess and think they could have done more. It's very difficult just to be at peace with doing your best under the given conditions of combat operations at night." Sean explained that despite having a primary job of being a medic the very nature of Kill/ Capture missions requires that secondary skills become primary and only when a teammate is badly hurt that you revert back to your primary skill set.

In all of this Sean eventually knew that he needed help and found me to help him with the trauma he had been exposed to throughout his career. Watching the movie American Sniper might give you an idea of what these men and women have to face but in many ways it's a simplified example of the multiple high level multi-tasking required of present day Special Operations and SWAT members. One can only imagine the stress this places on the body, as well as the human psyche in terms of the pain, grief, and survivor guilt they are often forced to process. Unique to Special Operations in many ways is the treatment of patients which are their friends and teammates. Sean was no exception to this. He had been self-medicating by using alcohol to sleep and tobacco to work the long hours. This combination also helped him to numb and avoid the pain he had been carrying while his emotional state had reached a boiling point. He had been keeping a lid on all of the frustration for years but it was beginning to boil over and bleed out into all areas of his life.

It's important to understand the context in which this population operates in order to truly appreciate how this approach was able to help him in ways that standard medical care and psychotherapy hadn't been able to do. This is a population that is more fearful of looking inside than going into a war zone. Their minds must continually wrestle and come to grips with what they had to do while at the same time being expected to be emotionally available and present for their families and those around them in the workplace. It is extremely difficult to go from active combat and war zones where total focus, anger, fear, and living 'on edge' serve as survival mechanisms to a civilian life where the space no longer requires the adrenaline rush and state of high alert which served them before. They now find themselves having to deal with and process a range of emotions such as pain, grief, sadness, and guilt that they've been holding down for far too long. Part of this means carrying and processing the deaths they were responsible for in a manner that doesn't weigh them down but actually supports them and gives them life. It was at this point when Sean came out to see me for his own personal healing journey.

Just as I do with all of my clients, I taught him a foundational breath technique that calms and eases the body allowing for fuller clarity and taught him how to ground and gain support through the earth. We then began the process of reconnecting him to a body that he had detached from long ago given the nature of his profession. In combat and war zones, the ability to detach and carry out the duties of the mission, which often includes killing enemy combatants, functions as a survival mechanism but when transitioning back into the new environment of civilian life, it works against them. I helped Sean get re-connected to his body and tap into his own intuition, something that had always been there but had been pushed down and ignored for years. In Sean's own words, this was the "game-changer, getting to the point where people start to listen to their body, their intuition and act on it with confidence." As we focused on the physical body, I helped him understand the changes his body not only went through during active combat but also through the transition to civilian life from a physiological and medical standpoint by helping him understand how his body's responses might be tied to neuro-limbic dysfunction, adrenal fatigue, and/or brain-gut connection, which then led to a referral to an integrative doctor.

On a mental and emotional level, we explored the deeper meaning through the body behind what was driving his frustration and anger. Sean had a tendency to put the interests of others, especially colleagues and managers in the professional realm, before himself, something that is not uncommon for this population. I had him bring his focus back to himself and gave him a toolkit of techniques and strategies on how to focus on the things he could control. Many of us try to 'fix' situations or change the needs and wants of others but most times the only thing we can do, and usually the best thing we can do, is focus on taking care of ourselves. This helped him understand where most of his anger and frustration was coming from and in his words allowed him to "meet his healing head on." He was able to dial back his anger and instead of going from, in his words, "0-100 mph," he now had the ability not to go full tilt all the time. He learned how to "find the message in the anger," which helped him moderate it back and deal with it in different ways.

As we worked through the underlying causes of his anger, we also worked through several deep layers of emotion his body was holding that had been stuffed down and ignored for years. I can tell you from working with thousands of clients with deep-seated trauma, especially those on the front lines of combat and war zones like Sean, peeling away the layers of emotional neglect can at times feel daunting. This gentle approach allows these individuals to stop punishing themselves and step into what has been suppressed without judgment. Finding the meaning and understanding through all of it, enables them to view their world and life in a new and positive way.

Since Sean's time with me and a few occasional tune-ups along the way, he reports being more emotionally available and present for his wife and kids and has learned to channel his frustration and anger in more constructive ways by finding the meaning behind it. Although he sometimes takes steps back, they aren't as severe or as long in duration. He continues to view things differently by looking at the underlying messages each situation is trying to teach him. Getting connected to his body held the key for doing so as he is now open to the messages it was holding about his anger and has learned how to connect and process the emotions of pain, grief, and guilt that were holding him back and keeping him stuck. As a result, he has become a strong supporter of the work I am doing and has been advocating for this type of treatment among his colleagues; an uphill battle for a group who is reluctant for personal and professional reasons to do so.

In terms of the professional reluctance, Sean pointed out that within the Secret Clearance renewal process, there is a box to check if the person has ever sought mental health care. As my work is not diagnosis-based and falls outside the bounds of standard mental health care, there is no conflict of interest with having to check that box when the clearance is up for reinvestigation. According to Sean, the current system discourages seeking mental health care especially for a population that critically needs it yet my treatment approach is an opportunity for this population to get the help they need without putting their professional career in jeopardy. Because of Sean's dedication and passion for helping others, especially those within this population, he felt it was important to share these words: "One of the things I've told someone who sought help from Paige is that there is light at the end of the tunnel. A little bit of light and hope instead of a freight train coming right at you. If it gets even one more person from our community to get help and not kill themselves, great. It's an epidemic and I'm happy to be part of the solution."

As both Erin and Sean struggled with traumatic situations involving death, grief, pain, and anger, my client Kelly, whose name has also been changed for privacy reasons, has been living with the death of a life she once had as she has been enduring a chronic medical condition that has not only affected her ability to work but also her ability to be there for her family. Kelly is a registered nurse who has been around enough patients to witness the pain, frustration and despair when a medical diagnosis for on-going symptoms cannot be found. Little did she know that this profession and experience with such cases would be preparing her for her eventual journey along a similar path. She, herself had endured decades of medical issues, such as hypothyroidism, irregular menstruation, mood changes, anger, depression, constant and severe migraines, difficulty regulating her body temperature, memory deficits and cognitive changes such as the inability to concentrate and being absentminded and forgetful. She suffered with low libido, sleep disturbances, weakness and dizziness, nausea, hypertension, and the inability to exercise, as well as severe bouts of anxiety with even the slightest amount of stress. After being rushed to the hospital this past New Year's Eve, an MRI finally revealed the cause of her symptoms. At age thirty-nine she was diagnosed with a

Rathke Cleft Cyst that had grown in her pituitary gland.

A year before her diagnosis, her level of functioning had severely declined. She began to experience intense nausea and was in an incredible amount of constant pain. She had a hard time performing simple tasks around the house like making meals for her family, laundry, cleaning, and writing emails. She also found it difficult to do many of the things she had always enjoyed such as communicating, laughing and finding joy, exercise, and physical activities that had once been part of her daily repertoire. Even walking around the block became too much. As you can imagine, this led to a painful period of guilt for her as she could no longer be the mother and wife she not only wanted to be but had once been.

The first time I met with Kelly, she wasn't able to fill out the paperwork as her anxiety was at an all-time high and her cognition wouldn't allow her to focus. Since the diagnosis, she had been in an excruciatingly painful period of having to wait to see medical specialists. Due to complex insurance issues, it would take her four months to meet with a surgeon to explore the potential steps of removing the cyst. All the while her fear continued to grow and her symptoms became worse.

As I did with Erin and Sean, I needed to help ground Kelly by teaching her foundational breathing techniques to help calm her system and lessen her anxiety. I then helped her re-connect to a body she felt had betrayed her so she could find comfort and get through moments of the day. After our first session together, she shared with me how she was able to do some things around the house and yard for the first time in a long while and was even able to enjoy an evening out with her husband. After a few more sessions, she began to go back to work slowly on a part-time basis working a few hours a week as she was now able to better mentally cope with the stress and demands of the job.

Through this illness and our work together, Kelly was beginning to understand what was occurring in her body and the underlying reasons why. She was beginning to hear the messages her body had been holding for her throughout her life and how these life stories from this lifetime and others had been playing out in her current life. This illness had gotten her attention in ways that wouldn't have been possible otherwise. It was now time for her to be open to these messages and really listen to what they were saying so she could move forward and grow on a much deeper level than she had ever imagined.

Early on in her sessions while she was still getting used to and learning the process, I had guided her to a certain place in her body that I knew needed her full attention. What she discovered began to change the course of her healing. Up until this point, she had questioned whether or not she had a strong will and the strength to live and survive. As we went into this particular place in her body, she not only realized she had it but allowed this realization to shift how she viewed her illness and the strength she would be able to use towards her recovery. The pain and discomfort in her body would inform her of the stories it had been holding for her personal growth and how to begin implementing information from them into her life. She became friendly with the dark night of her soul, not fearing it anymore and the messages it had for her. She was also able to understand how the cyst had lived before in her previous lifetimes and the unfinished business as to why it was still present in her current life.

As important as it was for Kelly to re-connect with her body and listen to the messages it was giving for her healing, it was equally important for her to know she was not alone on many levels. I validated for her that what she was going through was a very normal response to a life-changing illness. Many of my clients had experienced the same reactions and faced the same challenges so it was comforting for her to know she was not alone in this. I reminded her of the strong support system she already had in place and how this would help her through. I also brought in assistance from the other side. Interestingly, as the surgery date grew closer, Allison began showing up in our sessions letting Kelly know she was with her and would not be alone during the procedure. Once again, Allison would continue to work with me and through me for the benefit of my clients as her wings continue to inspire.

The work Kelly and I have been doing together has affected her on many levels. It has provided meaning and given her more of an understanding as to why this is happening in her life. She learned how to operate through the illness by going into her body and letting it tell her what she needs on a daily basis. She also began to learn how to reach out and ask for help and assistance; something that had always been uncomfortable for her to do. Because Kelly was someone who always put the needs of others before herself, she began to realize that she did not have to hold back her emotions and feelings with those close to her as she had every right to speak up about how this was affecting her. I remind her time and time again that living life, especially with a chronic illness, can't be done perfectly. It is very messy and she is fully justified to put aside the perfectionism and step into the messiness of it all. According to Kelly, one of her most profound moments was when she had an enormous amount of anxiety with her mind continually shouting the 'what if' questions. As she laid on the table with my hands at her heart center, I told her that there would be a message that she needed to hear. As she listened, a presence of peace came over her and pleaded for her to trust and to stop the questioning. It told her the surgery was the only option, it would go well, and she would finally get relief. At the time of this writing, Kelly had just undergone the surgery to remove the cyst and although the procedure was successful, there were some complications leaving her body in constant pain. Since the surgery, our sessions together have allowed me to provide emotional support while temporarily reducing the pain giving her body time to rest and recover. As her body recovers, the next part of her journey will be to continue listening to the messages her body will be sharing as she moves on to the next phase of her life.

Erin, Sean and Kelly each faced different life situations that got their attention by having them dig deep for personal growth, understanding, and meaning when all else felt helpless and hopeless. Whether it was through the traumatic death of a mother, the paradox of saving and taking lives, or enduring a life-long medical condition, there were two threads of similarity that ran through each of them. One was the thread of listening to the body to uncover the meaning behind the challenging situation and how to use this meaning for their own personal growth. The other was connecting them to those in their life who had transitioned. These experiences and the knowledge they have gained from them will be carried in their red bags as reminders of their personal growth and how this will someday assist others. These three individuals validate the messages deep within each of us and from beyond. Listen and let your body tell its story and be open to the messages outside this earthly realm.

13

INTEGRATION

The impact of traumatic situations, life-altering events and medical conditions, lives, breathes, and weaves its way through the fabric of our everyday lives. It doesn't discriminate as to who it touches as it finds its way to each and every one of us whether it occurs in our personal or professional lives or both. Think of the teachers who work with traumatized students and face the ongoing threat of school violence, especially in-school shootings, or the reporters, journalists, and TV anchors who have to write and report the traumatic events on a daily basis. Or think about our courtrooms where attorneys, judges, jurors, clerks, and administrative staff are continually exposed to the sordid details of horrific events and the all-too-familiar episodes of workplace violence, sexual harassment, and mass shootings that plague our society. And to all those on the front lines of stress and traumatic situations including our military and first responder populations, as well as doctors, nurses, and medical staff who have to make life-or-death decisions on a daily basis, finding meaning and, ultimately healing, from this can be overwhelming.

Beginning with my time in the ER as a young Candy Striper through my time in New York at Ground Zero to my current work helping clients deal with life-challenging situations, the theme of providing the best care to meet their individual needs, particularly with trauma and illness, has been my focal point. I learned through decades of working in the behavioral health field and the medical world, both personally and professionally, is that for optimal patient care to occur, there are some areas where improvements could be made. I would like to take this opportunity to share some thoughts on where and how to do so.

Having found success as a practitioner by creating a healing approach that relies on several modalities including some considered non-Western, I believe patient care could be improved if behavioral health providers were given the opportunities to expand their knowledge in several areas, including the medical field and alternative therapeutic modalities. Before they do so the CEU licensing boards, who govern the professional development opportunities, would have to expand its scope of oversight and be more open to a new vision for the future. The first step might be allowing CEUs for behavioral health providers to attend medical conferences so they can cross-train with medical personnel to better understand and recognize how mental and emotional components can manifest from an underlying medical condition. I've alluded to the brain-gut connection, adrenal fatigue, and neurotoxin illness but a more thorough understanding of medical illness and how it might serve as the origin for behavioral health symptomology would be beneficial. Trauma and chronic stress certainly create emotional distress and can be dealt with from a behavioral health standpoint but they can also stem from medical illness. Knowing the symptoms and becoming aware of how medical illness can mimic mental or emotional issues will not only change the way the practitioner interacts and treats the client or patient but will help to make the appropriate referrals for proper medical care.

Secondly, patient care outcomes can be improved if behavioral health practitioners incorporate modalities that might not fit the traditional Western paradigm. These modalities include energy medicine, yoga and yogic principles, Reiki, and Chinese medicine principles, along with two programs that I developed: Energetic Body Dialogue (EBD) and Biodynamic Touch Trauma Therapy (BTT). The integration of such modalities is gaining mainstream acceptance. According to an article in STAT, hospitals affiliated with Yale, Duke, Johns Hopkins and other top medical research centers, have been incorporating alternative healing modalities such as, homeopathy, Reiki, traditional Chinese herbal medicine, Intravenous vitamin and mineral therapies and natural and spiritual healing techniques into their practice.* This is not without controversy as some of the doctors interviewed for the article believe these practices are akin to "peddling snake oil" and medical professionals becoming "witch doctors" as they believe treatments that don't adhere to science-based evidence undermine the credibility of the institutions. The counter argument is that modern medicine has not and cannot provide a cure for everyone (i.e. multi-faceted complex illness). These hospitals and medical schools have decided to find what is best for the patient and say they are responding to the needs of the patients. According to the chief executive of the Cleveland Clinic Wellness Institute, Dr. Toby Cosgrove, "The old way of combating chronic disease hasn't worked . . . We have heard from our patients that they want more than conventional medicine can offer." In fact, according to the article, a national consortium to promote integrative health which had eight centers in 1999 is now up to seventy academic centers and health systems. It also notes

---

* www.statnews.com/2017/03/07/alternative-medicine-hospitals-promote/

the United States federal government spends close to $120 million a year to fund research through the NIH National Center for Complimentary and Integrative Health.

Last but not least, in the previous chapter I made the case for using the body's own innate wisdom and power to heal as a possible 'missing link' in the health and wellness field. Practitioners could learn how to help their clients tap into their inner wisdom and knowing and use the information the body is storing to help inform treatment. A noteworthy aspect to this approach is that it lets practitioners to conserve more of their own energy while still allowing the client to experience profound healing. The behavioral health providers I have trained in this methodology have in fact reported they have been able to conserve their energy and feel much less drained at the end of the client work day. Plus, it helps to empower the client or patient to have a stake and take ownership of his or her healing.

As I've shown throughout this book how it is that trauma-related and life-altering events impact our lives, I would be remiss if I didn't share how a more thorough understanding of these themes for medical providers would be another important facet leading to improved patient care. Cross-training medical providers from across the spectrum of the medical field could increase their repertoire and build a better understanding of how the emotional component of trauma, life-altering events and exposure to prolonged cumulative stress, often becomes lodged in the body and manifests itself through physical symptoms or disease. This includes examining the role of how various forms of stress and traumatic stress (i.e. acute, chronic, traumatic, complex, PTSD, etc.) relate to medical diagnoses and how, where, and why stress, trauma, and life-changing personal events affect the physical, emotional, energetic, mental and spiritual components of an individual.

Of equal importance to this clinical aspect is guiding these professionals through an in-depth examination of SELF to learn how this deeper connection leads to increased provider performance and improved patient care. There is a heavy emotional toll associated with having to confront and deal with life and death situations and conditions on a daily basis. Medical providers, like first responders, will often build a 'wall' between themselves and the patient in order to minimize this emotional burden and allow them to keep functioning without being completely saturated and overwhelmed by the traumatic and painful aspects of death, disease, and life tragedies. As much as this 'wall' serves to protect and insulate them from burning out, it can also serve to disconnect and possibly block them from providing the personal touch, kindness, and empathy most patients crave and need for optimal care. I have providers get in touch with their 'wall' and the emotions behind how it manifests both personally and professionally. An important aspect is figuring out how certain patients and situations act as personal triggers in their own lives. We learn how to recognize this and how to use this awareness not only for their own personal growth but also how to be more present for their patients.

Above all, there needs to be better communication and collaboration between the behavioral health and medical fields as they both inform and mirror each other. I say this both from a clinical and a personal perspective. In my own practice, I work collaboratively to share and refer clients with several integrative MDs, naturopaths and chiropractors who bring different pieces of the puzzle to the overall health and well-being of my clients. As Ken Jones mentioned in the Foreword, healing is a 'team sport.' From a personal perspective, nowhere was this more imperative than the approach my husband needed to utilize to rebuild himself back to health from his chronic illness. I exposed him to a broad array of healing practitioners and modalities and built a healing team that addressed every aspect of his physical, emotional, energetic, mental, medical, nutritional, and spiritual needs. The validation I seek for such an integrated approach lies no further than the man who has helped champion this book and has served as the inspiration for making it possible.

14

FINAL THOUGHTS

When you think about your life, I bet there have been times when things occur which you cannot explain yet somehow validate or ring true for what you needed at a particular time. How does that happen you may ask? The bigger question is how could it not happen since we are all connected to each other, the land, its animals, and everything else that vibrates in this world and beyond. We can never know all of the reasons why something tragic, challenging, or painful happens in our lives.

What I have come to see and learn is that within it all, there are messages that come from within and from beyond, giving us inner peace and letting us know that we are not alone. I wish I had the answers to piece the full puzzle of the unknown together but I don't. I know for me I am given pieces of the big picture that I pass along to others who may also have pieces that I do not, yet time and time again, there appears to be a similarity and validation of the pieces I and others are given. These similarities continue to validate that we are so much more than just human beings and that we are supported from beyond this earthy realm in more ways than one. I know that for me, I am here to assist individuals through their challenging journeys while also teaching those out there all I have learned that can be useful to them in their everyday professional approaches to wellness.

I believe the world we live in is one pit stop on our journey to many other worlds. Who's to say that we are not living parallel lives all at the same time or that so much of what goes on here is just an illusion? We will fully know when we transition from our physical body, but until such time I urge you to dig into your red bag, keep what serves you and release what doesn't, and share and pass along to others what is purposeful and helpful and always be open to the messages both from within and beyond this earthly realm.

In Appreciation

There are many people to thank when a book finally comes to fruition as it is a project that I could not have completed on my own.

I thank Jan Henrikson for being the editor and person who came and sat on my couch, laptops in hand for eight months asking questions and pulling out of me the ideas, information, and stories for this book. Her energy and support was the much-needed catalyst to get the book moving.

I thank Richard Fenwick for not only laying out the insides of the book in a way that is easy and inviting for the reader but for the support and guidance he patiently gave me on this project.

To the clients of mine who were courageous enough to tell their stories in the book so that readers could see that even in the darkest of nights, light still does shine through and meaning does rise up. I thank you!

To my friend and mentor, Phyl for your ongoing kindness and support as we both travel in a world that may not be fully ready for what we represent.

A special thank you to Allison's family for allowing me to share the intimate details of the journey their beautiful daughter and sister had with me and how she continues to touch my life and others from beyond this earthly realm.

Most importantly a special warm and loving thank you to Wanda, Allison's mother whose honest and revealing chapter about her personal journey throughout and after her daughter's transition will help many who are struggling every day with the loss of their child.

Many thanks to Sarah O'Neill and Emily Halbert for assisting me in creating and implementing a one-of-a-kind book cover that truly emanates the depth and meaning of this book. You both brought different skills and talents that created a superb combination and I couldn't be more pleased and grateful for your time and patience in this very personal project.

Lastly and most importantly to my mother who gave me life. I thank you for opening yourself up to reliving, writing, and talking about the first year of my life that almost ended yours. Working with you on the chapter brought me a clearer understanding of how the dots connected for my life purpose. I enjoyed our time working together in bringing to life an experience and message that can be passed along to others in hopes of assisting in their lives. I love you mom!!

ABOUT PAIGE

Paige Valdiserri is an internationally recognized Traumatic Stress an Integrative Healing Consultant. Her international work at the corporate level, which includes programs in the Middle East and Africa, and her unique integrative healing approach have empowered thousands of individuals on the front lines of stress to go from a place of personal fracturing back to a state of wholeness.

As a Board-Certified Expert in Traumatic Stress, Paige is also a Licensed Professional Counselor, Energy Medicine Healer, Biodynamic Craniosacral Trauma Therapist, Body Therapist, Master Reiki Teacher, Shamanic healer, Spiritual intuitive, Kundalini Yoga instructor, clairvoyant, empath and body intuitive. Her professional experience includes the fields of education, behavioral health, and health & wellness, as well as corporate and government where she worked with military, first responders, and contracted personnel.

Her speaking engagements and keynote addresses include the Arizona Fire District Association, the National Association of State Women Veterans Coordinators, Inc., the American Counseling Association, and Georgetown University's symposium "Every Crisis is a Human Crisis." She also addressed the Defense Health Board Task Force on Mental

Health as a panel expert and was featured as the keynote speaker for NASA's Executive Safety Forum.

Paige consults and collaborates with physicians, chiropractors, and integrative holistic practitioners around the country through live video chats, workshops, teleconferences, podcasts and patient care to integrate her work into the medical and behavioral health fields.

Her first book, *Messages from the Edge: Paigeisms for Transformational Healing*, is dedicated to anyone who has struggled or is struggling with life's challenges and traumas, or who is committed to their own self-growth and discovery. You can learn more about Paige at *www.paigevaldiserri.com*.